KNOWABOUT
BASKETBALL

Chris Bunnett and Sean McSweeney

Produced by AA Publishing

Cover: a perfect one-handed dunk by A.C. Green
(Allsport Photographic)
Title page: Michael Jordan of Chicago Bulls in action
(Allsport Photographic)

Written by Chris Bunnett and Sean McSweeney

Photography: Allsport Photographic
Illustrations: Oxford Illustrators Ltd.

Typesetting by Microset Graphics Ltd., Basingstoke
Repro by Scantrans Pte Ltd., Singapore
Printed and bound by L.E.G.O. SpA, Italy

Produced by AA Publishing

Published by The Automobile Association,
Fanum House, Basing View, Basingstoke,
Hampshire RG21 2EA

ISBN: 0 7495 0153 7

A CIP catalogue record for this book is available
from the British Library.

CONTENTS

FOREWORD

When you pick up a ball you find the most natural thing in the world is to bounce it, throw it, and catch it. I think the key to basketball's popularity is to be found in the fact that these fundamental skills, combined with the equally natural recreational activities of running and jumping, form the basis of the game. Add the magic ingredient of competition, and you have a sport in which the participants cannot help but get involved totally. At its highest level, basketball is a game of great athleticism, sustained effort, and determined rivalry; but there is also evidence of subtle skill, finesse, intelligence and sportsmanship. All of these facets of the game start to emerge as the beginner comes to grips with the sport.

I have had the good fortune to be involved in basketball since my schooldays. Later, as a Physical Training Instructor, I played for the British Army and Combined Services team, before moving on to coaching, spending three enjoyable years as a basketball specialist at Aldershot, England, where I combined teaching with research. I also took up officiating, and in the last 10 years I have been lucky enough to referee many top-level international service games, including the Supreme Headquarters of Allied Powers in Europe (SHAPE) Final in Belgium for three consecutive years.

My interest in the sport continues to grow. Although the game's principles are simple, the higher the level, the more complex and interesting the tactics become. Basketball integrates individual skills into a team effort.

Beginners will find the basic skills explained with step-by-step diagrams and text, before being introduced to more advanced techniques. Each skill has a difficulty rating, shown by the small basketball players at the top of each page. One player indicates that the skill is relatively easy to acquire, whereas three show a technique that is more difficult to perfect. Don't be tempted to rush each stage; it's far better (and often safer) to lay down a good foundation. The sections on "defence" and "attack", rules and scoring put this in the context of a team sport, and the action studies show how the theory is put into practice in top-class competition. You can improve your standard by following the fitness and training sections and the graduated tests.

Readers already acquainted with the game of basketball can always benefit from a review of basics and they, as well as those who work through the first sections of this book, will benefit from the STAR TIPS — sound advice that top players give, and which can add that little bit extra to your game.

In my travels as player, coach and official I have experienced and witnessed the pleasure basketball can bring, and I will feel I have given something back to the sport if, through this book, I can persuade you to take up the game. Who knows, one day, you may find yourself lifting a major trophy — like Dino Radja of the Yugoslavian team Yugoplastika.

Chris Bunnett

Victory in the European basketball final: Dino Radja holds the cup for Yugoslavian team Yugoplastika

INTRODUCTION

When, in 1891, Dr. James Naismith, a lecturer in an American college, devised a game that would keep his students fit during the winter months, he surely could have had no idea what he was starting. Today, the game of basketball is played all over the world — by boys, girls, men and women — at many different levels. Professionals and amateurs compete at local, national and international level. Basketball attracts wide sponsorship and enthusiastic audiences and has long been a fully recognised Olympic sport. (In the interests of clarity and simplicity, the basketball player is referred to as "he" in the main text of this book.)

Needless to say, the game of basketball has undergone many changes in the last century — how different it is from the "ball and ring" games which are known to have been popular in the ancient civilisations of Central and South America — but many of the basic principles remain the same. True, it is no longer possible, as Dr. Naismith envisaged, for as many as 50 players to participate, nor would many of today's competitors be happy to play on an uneven surface if that were the only one available. But the game is still based on the ideal of no contact between opposing players, with grace, agility and "physical judgement" as prime attributes, and each team still attempting to move the ball into their opponents' territory where they can throw it into their basket. Perhaps the most beneficial innovation has been the continuous dribble; no other aspect of the game so contributes to its fluidity and dynamism.

Basketball is an exciting, all-action sport with rules which ensure that it is an attacking game. And although there are advantages to height in a game where the target is 10ft (3m) off the ground, the popular image of the tall, lean basketball player need not discourage anyone, since there is always room for a quick-witted, skilful, smaller player. There are several on some of the top teams.

Different versions of the game, with slightly modified equipment, have been developed to encourage the game among very young children. There is also Wheelchair Basketball which is played all over the world. Basketball is for everyone. Start here to find out why it is for you.

KEY TO DIAGRAM 2
(International backboard, basket and net measurements)
A 1ft 11in (0.59m)
B 1ft 6in (0.45m)
C 5ft 11in (1.80m)
D 3ft 11in (1.20m)
E 1ft 6in (0.45m)
F 1ft 4in (0.40m)
G 6in (0.15m)
H 1ft (0.30m)

[1] To begin with, a hard, even surface and a ring at a suitable height (preferably with a backboard) will suffice to introduce you to the basics of the game, but you will soon need to get acquainted with the standard court. It should have a hard surface which gives an even bounce; the traditional material is wood, but other coverings are also used. Many courts are indoors and need to be well-lit. The restricted area (also known as the key) found at each end of the court includes the semi-circle which extends from its narrower end. The circle of which it forms part is the same size as the centre circle and, like it, is known as a restraining circle. The arc which is 21ft (6.4m) away from the basket is the three-point line. The purpose of all these markings will become clear later in the book.

[2] The backboard stands 4ft (1.2m) in from the end line; here are its measurements and those of the basket and net it supports.

[3] In the US National College Athletics Association (NCAA) League the restricted area and three-point line have the appearance and dimensions shown in diagram 3. Diagram 1 and all other court illustrations in this book show international markings.

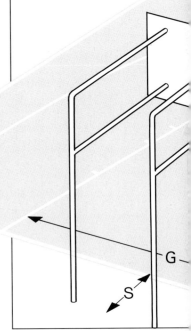

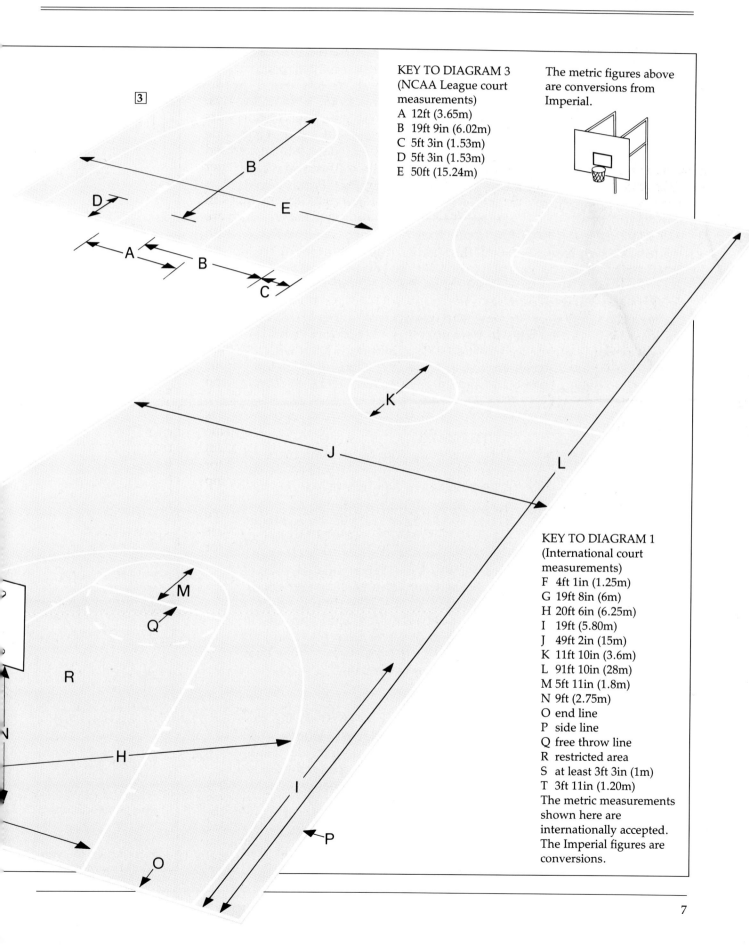

KEY TO DIAGRAM 3
(NCAA League court measurements)
A 12ft (3.65m)
B 19ft 9in (6.02m)
C 5ft 3in (1.53m)
D 5ft 3in (1.53m)
E 50ft (15.24m)

The metric figures above are conversions from Imperial.

KEY TO DIAGRAM 1
(International court measurements)
F 4ft 1in (1.25m)
G 19ft 8in (6m)
H 20ft 6in (6.25m)
I 19ft (5.80m)
J 49ft 2in (15m)
K 11ft 10in (3.6m)
L 91ft 10in (28m)
M 5ft 11in (1.8m)
N 9ft (2.75m)
O end line
P side line
Q free throw line
R restricted area
S at least 3ft 3in (1m)
T 3ft 11in (1.20m)
The metric measurements shown here are internationally accepted. The Imperial figures are conversions.

EQUIPMENT AND CLOTHING

You might start by playing basketball very informally — a few practice sessions with friends, and the occasional game among yourselves. In which case, ordinary tennis shoes, gym socks, shorts (with a support worn underneath for men and boys) and a T-shirt will be suitable clothing. It is also a good idea to have a tracksuit to wear during the warm-up and at the end of a game as you cool down, or to wear in cold halls and gymnasiums; this is one of the easiest ways to avoid chills and soft-tissue injuries. Even if you are starting to play the game, it is advisable to play with a standard size ball — smaller sizes are available for young children.

As you progress, you should purchase a pair of proper basketball shoes (see picture 2). Good, thick socks of absorbent fabric are also important. If you start playing on a team, you will need proper sleeveless team vests with numbers on the back and front. Each player has a different number.

From the safety point of view, soft contact lenses are preferable to glasses. If glasses have to be worn, they should have plastic lenses in sturdy plastic frames and be tied around the head with a strong elastic band. Jewellery and watches can be hazardous to the wearer and other players, and should be removed before the start of the game.

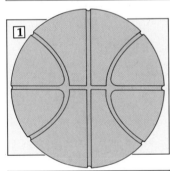

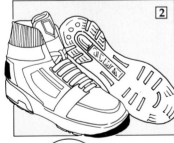

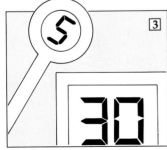

1 THE BALL

This is round, with a circumference of about 30in (76cm) and a diameter of 9in (22cm). Balls can be made of leather, rubber or other suitable synthetic materials. Those made from rubber or synthetic materials are cheaper and will last longer on rough outdoor surfaces — so they are ideal for beginners. When inflated, the ball weighs between 21 and 23oz (595-650g), and the top of the ball should reach a height of between 4ft (1.2m) and 4ft 7in (1.4m) when dropped from 6ft (1.8m) off the ground (the distance between the floor and the bottom of the ball).

2 SHOES

Shoes must have good grips on the sole and strong laces of adequate length. They must fit well and be comfortable. High-tops, which protect and support the ankle, are preferable to low-cut shoes.

3 OTHER EQUIPMENT

Among the equipment needed at a higher level are score sheets, clocks and foul markers for the scorers.

ANKLE PROTECTION
Jay Humphries of Phoenix Suns moves threateningly into the opponents' key. Professionals often wear supports on their knee and ankle joints, as much to prevent injury as to protect an existing one. Even the casual or amateur player should consider wrapping or taping the ankle joints, but only after expert advice, to limit the strain that can be caused by constant jumping and turning.

 STAR TIPS
Sweatbands on the wrist can help keep the ball dry to ensure good handling, and can be used to wipe sweat out of your eyes as you prepare to take that vital free throw. Wear an extra pair of socks to prevent blistering — and remember to wear two pairs when you try on new shoes in a shop.

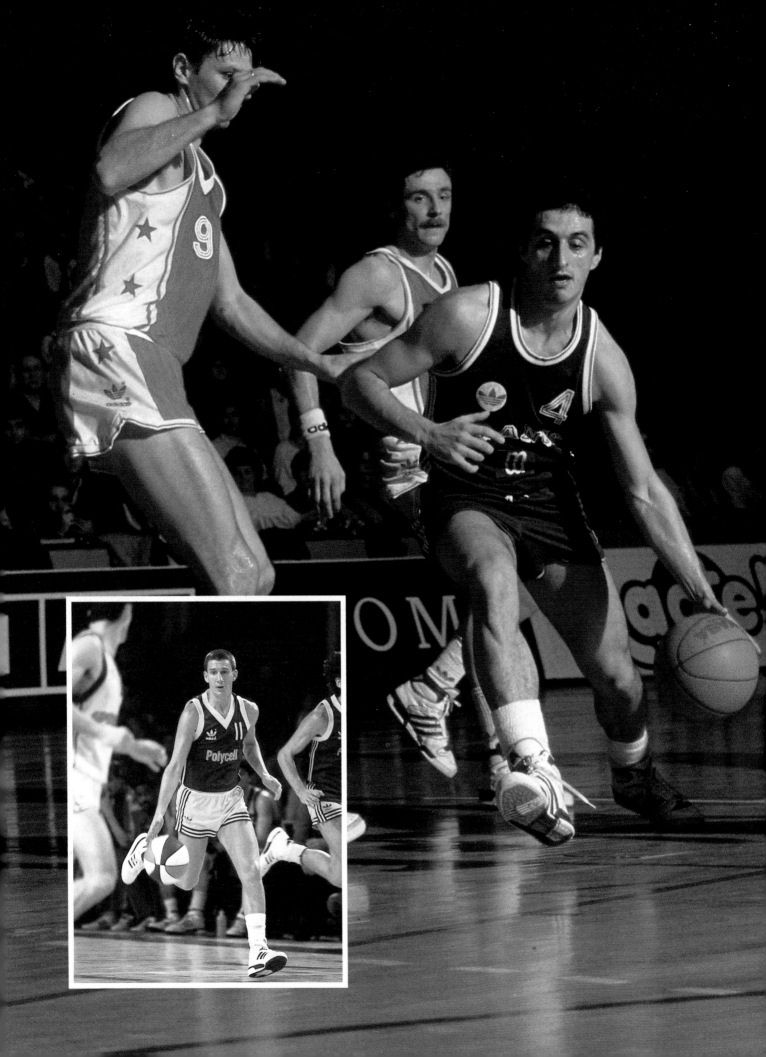

DRIBBLING (1)

Obviously the quickest way of moving the ball from one end of the basketball court to the other is by passing it from player to player. However, this is not always possible. If you are coming out of defence, your team-mates might not yet be in suitable positions to receive a pass; and while you are building an attack, the opposition might be doing a good job of restricting the options open to you. This is where dribbling is so important − it allows you to buy time until a passing or shooting opportunity presents itself; it unsettles defenders by forcing them to watch both the ball and the players they are guarding; and, if done skilfully, it can allow you to penetrate the defence directly and get a shot from close in.

A dribbler who makes full use of both hands, who knows how to shield the ball, and who can change direction quickly and smoothly, is hard to "steal" from, and will often draw more than one defender towards him, thereby releasing a team-mate for a pass − in which case, he *should* pass. This brings us to an important point about this valuable skill: it should always be *purposeful*. Since the rules state that a team must make an attempt on the basket within 30 seconds of getting the ball, or else lose possession, it is easy to see how a selfish player can cost his team valuable time and scoring opportunities.

THE PROTECTED DRIBBLE
A beautifully controlled low dribble by Hufnagel of France. Things to note: the head is in a vertical plane with the eyes looking straight ahead (not at the ball), the knees are well flexed as he takes a good stride to go past his opponent who is already in a poor position to stop him. His body is between the ball and the defender and he has his right arm up for extra protection.
INSET: under less immediate pressure, Steve Bontrager, of the British team Kingston, moves out of defence with a relaxed and more upright dribble. Again he looks straight ahead, working out the possibilities.

 STAR TIP
The low dribble is the first one you should learn. To get used to not looking at the ball, practise with a friend who will hold up some fingers on his hand and ask you to say how many he is showing.

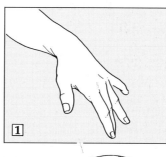

STEP 1
Use the top joints of the fingers and thumb (*not* the palm of the hand) to control the ball. The whole movement should be fairly relaxed, the main effort coming from the wrist and fingers, with only a small amount of elbow action. The upper arm is more or less in line with the body. As the ball goes down, the fingers momentarily point to the floor.

STEP 2
The wrist straightens and the hand comes up to control the ball as it rises. As the ball touches the fingertips, let the hand and forearm rise with the ball to cushion the impact before guiding the ball downwards again.

STEP 3
The correct stance: body leaning forwards, knees bent, one foot in front of the other, head held up and eyes looking straight ahead, the upper body crouched (but not hunched up) over the ball. This position will vary slightly according to the type and speed of the dribble.

DRIBBLING (2)

All the handling skills in basketball should be practised so that you are competent and confident using either hand; this is never truer than when dribbling the ball. Defenders will soon detect a player who can only dribble on one side and they will find it easy to steer him away from the basket or even steal the ball from him. Dribble with the right hand when going to the right and use your left hand when moving left. By switching hands at the right time you can shield the ball from the defence by keeping your body between ball and opponent. Watch the top players and note all the different ways in which they dribble — sometimes bouncing the ball from hand to hand between their legs or behind their back. They don't do this to show off (well, not entirely!), but to protect the ball from the opposing defenders. Note also the different ways they move about the court as they dribble: running, walking, turning, shuffling, even standing still. Each type of dribble is suited to a particular situation and purpose.

Let's now look at a type of dribble which is used when the ball is driven out of defence at speed and there is no immediate need to shield the ball — the high dribble. For good measure we will include a switch of hands. Never, by the way, bounce the ball with two hands at once; this is equivalent to a catch and brings the dribble to an end.

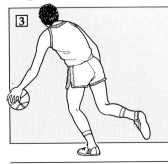

STEP 1

Only run at a speed which will allow you to control the ball. With practice you can get faster, but bear in mind that you may have to slow down or change direction suddenly. A full, running stride is used and the ball is pushed further in front of your body than it would be in a low dribble, with the result that your dribbling arm is more extended. The wrist and finger technique is as described on page 11 but, as greater force is needed, there will be more elbow action. The top of the bounce will come between the waist and the shoulder.

STEP 2

To switch hands, push the ball across the front of the body (the cross-over) but not so far ahead that you invite a steal. The right leg is forward as you switch from right to left, and the left leg forward for the opposite change.

STEP 3

You should perform the whole movement smoothly without slowing down. The dribble now continues on the other side.

THE HIGH DRIBBLE
Both feet off the ground as he drives forward in full stride, Michael Jackson of the Sacramento Kings is in full control of this high dribble. His head is perfectly poised and his upper body leans forwards into the sprint.

 STAR TIP
Clyde Drexler of Portland Trail Blazers (INSET) demonstrates an important point as he drives into the opposition's territory. His head is tilted down, but he is not looking at the ball; this is a way of increasing your peripheral vision to the side and slightly behind you, and of checking on opponents approaching from areas you would not normally see.

DRIBBLING (3)

1 – 4 Any dribble, regardless of its type, must be controlled. This sequence shows the value of low and protected dribbling.

1 This junior player is moving in towards the 3-point line when he finds himself closely guarded by a quick-footed defender. Note how the dribbler turns his body into the defender and keeps the ball as far away from him as possible.

2 The dribbler is looking for players he can pass to, but no help is available. He keeps his arm up to help protect the ball, which is now almost behind his back.

3 & 4 The dribbler is forced to retreat. He moves backwards while looking ahead to see if he can pass. The defender shows good footwork and determined defence but the attacker's dribble is smooth and controlled, and he keeps possession despite losing ground. At no time in this sequence does the dribbler look at the ball. A great deal of practice and match play has gone into making his dribble automatic. He can maintain it while concentrating on the movement of the players off the ball.

5 Among the things to note in this more aggressive example of dribbling from Terry Porter of Portland is the way the player is shielding the ball from the defender as he goes past him. The drive is not as open as the examples we saw on page 13. To find the reason for this, look at the floor beneath his feet. Many top courts have the key painted a different colour (yellow in

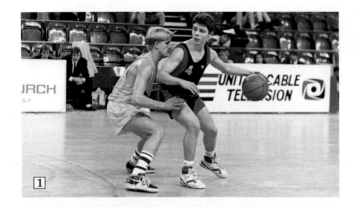

this case) from the rest of the floor. Since members of the attack may only stay in the key for up to 3 seconds, the ball handler must be extremely conscious of his position on the court. As Terry Porter is planning to shoot, the defenders are forcing him to protect the ball.

6 Quick change of pace and direction have taken Michael Jorden, of the Chicago Bulls, past his opponent. Once a dribbler has his head and shoulders past a defender, the defender cannot stop him without fouling, unless he gets in front of him again.

7 Here we have a drag dribble. The attacker is using a fairly low dribble and is working her way to the opponents' key (you can just see the lines painted in blue) by turning her back on her defender and taking side-steps. You need to be able to turn neatly to attack the basket from this type of dribble.

6

11 Here is a good, high, driving dribble by a member of the Northampton (England) team. A sudden change of direction has left the defender facing the wrong way and her left arm is angled to push the ball well in front of her body to maintain the speed of her run. (This photo was taken at the 1989 Women's National Basketball Championship.)

11

7

8 – **10** Andrew Bailey of Brixton Topcats (England) moves towards the 3-point line. He is driving, but is crouched low so that the ball doesn't bounce high enough for a defender to get a steal.

He gets past one opponent, shielding the ball nicely, but runs into more, so decides to play a bounce pass into the edge of the key to a team-mate.

8

9

10

THE STANCE

When playing basketball you should always be prepared, even if you are not involved directly in the action. The game is a fast one, played on a small court — which can seem even smaller when you are under pressure — and you are never more than a long throw away from the ball. Defence can become attack in one swift move and you may suddenly find yourself having to respond to a totally new threat. Moreover, basketball is a game in which the team tends to move as a unit. If a team-mate is attacking, you will be in your opponent's half of the court to support the move. If the opposition has the ball, your prime responsibility will be to defend and win the ball back — even if you are your team's best shooter.

Concentration, then, is important whether the ball is in your hands or someone else's. When you don't have the ball, study the play and be prepared to move quickly to help your team, or to hinder the efforts of your opponents, and remember that the ball might come your way at any time.

Anticipation and awareness are of little use, however, if your stance does not allow your body to respond to the orders which your mind gives it. At a split-second's notice you may be called on to jump, sidestep, sprint, turn or catch. The correct basic stance will enable you to perform these actions.

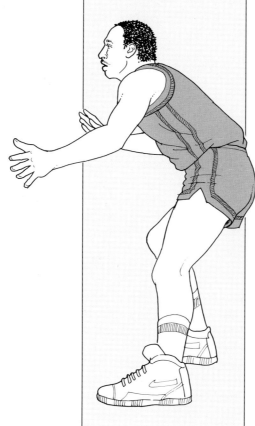

THE DEFENSIVE STANCE
The defensive stance is quite a variation on the basic one. Here we see James Worthy of the Lakers confronting his Milwaukee opponent. The stance is low with the arms out to prevent a dribble or pass. The legs are wide apart, feet firmly on the ground, knees bent. The player is coiled, ready to move in any direction.
INSET: Adrian Dantley of the Utah Jazz finds himself facing the stance which is used when the attacker is holding the ball high. The arm nearer the ball is up to prevent a shot or high pass, the other arm is down to counter the threat of a low pass.

THE BASIC STANCE
Stand with one leg a little in front of the other and your knees slightly flexed. Your balance should be such that you can move into any of the very different actions mentioned above with equal ease and effectiveness; to ensure that this is so, distribute your body weight evenly by placing your feet approximately shoulder-width apart. The upper body will be inclined slightly forwards. Face the action with your head held naturally, ready to move your whole body if the focus of play shifts to another part of the court.

You don't normally run, catch or jump with your arms hanging straight down by your sides, so there is no advantage to be gained by keeping them there. Your arms should be bent, but not rigid, with your hands at hip height, just in front of the body.

The basic stance is taken up by most people quite naturally when they are concentrating on the game. The secret is to be both relaxed and alert, and this will enable you to make sudden movements on court without strain or clumsiness.

FOOTWORK: THE PIVOT

Basketball is a game of almost perpetual motion, and the footwork used is extremely varied. Defenders have to keep pace with attackers and try to keep them away from the basket. Attackers try to outwit the defenders by varying their pace and direction. The basic stance (pages 16-17), with the knees flexed, makes it easy to launch into a run, although trying to stop is more often a problem. Play tends to concentrate at either end of the court with all the players very near each other and, with physical contact between opponents outlawed, you will appreciate the value of being able to stop quickly. This is even harder to do if you are concentrating on catching or dribbling the ball. Always move at an appropriate speed, bearing in mind the circumstances of the moment. Coming out of defence, a full sprint is often possible, but moving into a crowded front court requires more care. In a sense, you are rather like a car in traffic; to drive fast on a congested street is asking for trouble.

Another rule which underlines the importance of stopping quickly is the one which prohibits walking or running with a held ball. A player ending a dribble or catching the ball while on the move must do so in one stride or else release the ball. Once he has stopped, however, he may pivot. This is a very useful skill.

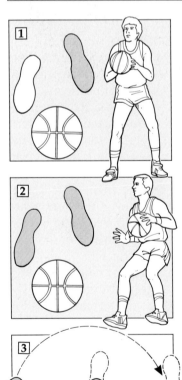

STEP 1
Before being able to pivot you must stop running. Here, having caught the ball, you ground one foot (shaded), in this case the left one. Count "one". The right foot comes through as the left knee bends to help you brake.

STEP 2
The right foot now lands. Count "two". This is known as the "stride stop" and the back foot can act as a pivot. If you manage to hit the ground with both feet at the same time (the "jump stop"), as you might from a rebound, you may use either foot as the pivot — but cannot change once you have chosen the pivot foot.

STEP 3
The pivot means that you can swivel on the ball of the back foot either to the left or right, giving you a whole circle of potential movement. This can be used to change the direction you are facing, to protect the ball from an opponent, or to fake a pass, shot or dribble. Be warned, though — a closely guarded player holding the ball must pass, shoot or start a dribble within 5 seconds.

PIVOTING INTO THE PASS
British League Star Micah Blunt swivels on the ball of his left foot into a position where a pass is possible. The Bayern Leverkusen (Germany) defender has his arms held high, which has left a passing lane open for the Kingston player to bounce a pass off the right hip.

 STAR TIP
If Micah Blunt had simply pivoted into the position, he would have found the defender blocking his path. You can fake before pivoting when you are closely guarded; if the fake is successful, you will have that half second of freedom from the defender in which to make your move count.

FOOTWORK IN PRACTICE

1

2

STAR TIP

With a friend practise catching the ball as you land on one foot ("count of one"). Your second foot will land ("count of two") and you should then turn, using the back foot as the pivot, and repeat the exercise in the opposite direction. Do not always use the same foot on the count of one.

3 This picture shows Demory of France executing a similar move to Joe Wolf's, but this time you get an overhead view. The footwork of Russia's Miglinieks (on the left) is worth studying; he is moving back with the attacker, trying to obstruct his progress without making contact. He is in a position where he can take a long sideways or backward stride. His stance would be improved by having his arms up and out, instead of by his sides.

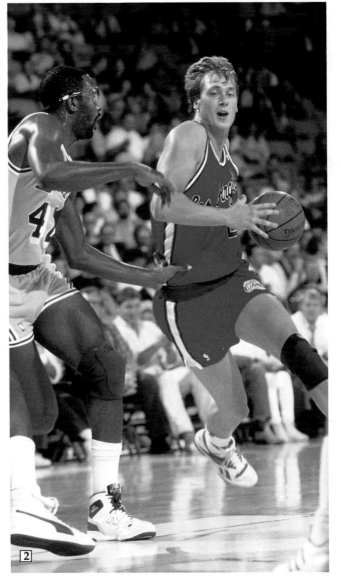

1 Eric "Sleepy" Floyd of the Houston Rockets is seen here on the "count of one" in his stride. He has just taken the ball in his hands, almost certainly from his own dribbling (his eyes are still looking ahead), and when his front foot comes down he will have to pass or shoot because, at the speed he is going, he certainly won't be able to stop!

2 Joe Wolf of the Los Angeles Clippers still has a "count of two" left – but he will also have to release the ball. Note the sharp angle at which he runs across the court to shield the ball from the defence. In photos 1 and 2 both players demonstrate confident footwork and good balance.

3

5

4

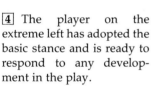

6

4 The player on the extreme left has adopted the basic stance and is ready to respond to any development in the play.

5 An example of good defensive footwork by this member of the English wo-men's team, Crystal Palace. She has stepped across to hinder the attacker and her left arm is raised to block the shot. Side-stepping is an important part of defence; it enables the defender to keep close to a dribbler and change direction if neces-sary. The feet are not lifted very high off the floor. When the trailing foot lands, you push off it and the leading foot stretches out sideways, in the direction you are going. The trailing foot will follow naturally.

6 Here we see the disad-vantage of jumping too soon. The defender has fallen for a fake by Anita Curtis of Northampton (England). She has leapt to block a shot or high pass which now allows the attacker to dribble or play a low pass. If you receive the ball while standing still or stopping and are confronted by a defender, the stance Anita Curtis has taken up gives the greatest choice of action. Crouch low, feet apart, and hold the ball about 9in (23cm) in front of your stomach. From here you can dribble, pass or shoot — so it is known as the triple-threat position. The defender has to be prepared to counter all three.

HANDLING AND CATCHING

There is nothing more discouraging than good, well-planned play being ruined by someone missing a catch or losing control of the ball while shooting. Good ball handling creates confidence within a team, which is almost like having an extra player. If the opposition knows that everyone on your side has good enough reactions and ball handling skills to make a steal and set up a counter-attack, they will be unlikely to try adventurous moves; and a predictable enemy is easier to contain.

Fortunately, you don't need a gym or a partner to practise the skills you need. To practise catching, bounce the ball off a wall at varying speeds and angles. If you can practise with a friend, then make the throws progressively more difficult to catch — you won't always get ideal passes in a match.

Get familiar with the feel and weight of the ball — use your imagination. Move the ball all the way round your body without it touching the ground, pass it from hand to hand under your legs and behind your head. Then try it with your eyes shut. You will notice how it feels in the pads of the fingers, which really give you control over the ball. Different shots and passes require the ball to be held in slightly different ways, and you should become familiar with all of them.

STEP 1
You can help the passer by signalling to tell him (a) that you are ready to accept a pass and (b) where you want him to throw the ball. Watch the ball all the way — this holds true for a pass, an interception, a rebound or a loose ball. Not only will it help you assess the flight of the ball so that you can position yourself early, it will also enable you to spot any deflection which might make the ball difficult to catch.

STEP 2
Use both hands where possible. The arms are stretched out, the elbows in close to the body, and the fingers spread with the thumbs positioned so that they will be behind the ball. You will almost always move towards the ball, even if it is coming straight to you. If the pass is inaccurate or if you are intercepting, you may have to take several steps.

STEP 3
As you catch the ball, relax your elbows and bring the ball in towards your body to absorb the impact. Don't let the ball slap into your palms.

CATCHING THE BALL
John Johnson of Bayern Leverkusen (Germany) prepares to receive a pass. His feet are spread apart to give him a firm base as he watches the ball on its way into his hands. His elbows are in, so that his thumbs are positioned to grip the back of the ball. His hands are nicely apart with the fingers spread to provide a firm grip. With a stance like this, you should never drop a catch.
INSET: an excellent example of taking a catch on the run. The Oslo player already knows what is in front of her so she can watch the ball with confidence as it comes to her out of defence. Again, look at the wide spread of the hands.

PASSING: THE CHEST PASS

Passing is a skill that must be performed well by every player on the basketball court. A team that cannot pass the ball properly will get very few opportunities to score — it's as simple as that. A good pass will be:

- accurate: the receiver shouldn't have to stretch or strain to catch the ball;
- at the correct speed: it should be fast enough to prevent any opponents from intercepting it, but not so fast that your team-mate cannot control it;
- well-timed: if a team-mate gets free, pass to him before the defender recovers and guards him again;
- appropriate: each type of pass is correct for a specific situation; you must choose the right one.

In addition to these general principles, certain other points should be made. First, pass using two hands whenever possible; you will find you have more control over the speed and direction of the ball. As for dribbling and catching, the fingers should be well spread. Second, be aware of the positions of other members of your team; are you giving the ball to the player who is best placed to create a scoring chance? Third, remember there is nothing to be gained by passing to someone who is not expecting the ball. Finally, don't forget that the simplest pass is usually the best.

STEP 1
The chest pass is the safest and simplest pass in basketball. The ball is held just in front of the lower half of the chest, elbows tucked in, thumbs behind the ball, fingers spread on the sides of the ball. The head and shoulders lean towards the target, and the knees are slightly bent. The wrists are cocked; the "snap" which occurs when they straighten is what drives the ball to its target.

STEP 2
Step forwards as you extend your arms and push with wrists, thumbs and fingers to propel the ball. This step makes passing easier but isn't always possible in a match, so practise with feet together as well. Aim for the receiver's chest and try to make the flight of the ball as horizontal as possible.

STEP 3
The follow-through should end with your thumbs pointing at the floor and your palms facing the receiver. This pass is the ideal one to make straight from a catch to a team-mate who is not closely guarded.

THE CHEST PASS
Reggie Theus of the Sacramento Kings sends a pass to a team-mate several yards away. The follow-through, with the fingers facing down, is unorthodox and suggests that he has looped the ball slightly upwards with lots of back-spin. The heel of his back foot is off the ground, evidence that he has stepped into the pass.

PASSING: THE PUSH PASS

As you gain experience in passing the ball, you will discover more ways of making things difficult for the opposition. One trick which can be applied to every area of the sport is the "fake", in which you make your opponent believe you are going to do something and, once he has committed himself to preventing it, then make another completely different move. Before passing the ball, pretend to shoot or start a dribble or deceive him about the type of pass or its direction. It is important that once you fool an opponent you take immediate advantage of the chance to pass. Disguising your intentions is even easier if you can acquire the knack of passing to a team-mate without even looking at him. The peripheral vision which allows you to dribble the ball without looking directly at it will also enable you to look at one person and throw the ball accurately to someone else. This is something you can practise with a friend.

The wider the range of passes at your disposal, the greater a threat you will be, especially if you can do one-handed passes, like the push pass, with either hand. In a match, improvisation can be important, but save your fancy passes for practice sessions until you have perfected them. One final point: when you have passed the ball, don't just stand there and admire your handiwork — move! Get into a position to support the attack.

THE PUSH PASS
John Johnson of Bayern Leverkusen (Germany). Look at the wide barrier presented by Brian Smith, who is No. 24 in the opposing team, to the left of Johnson. The Leverkusen player seems completely relaxed as he prepares to pass.

 STAR TIP

Magic Johnson (INSET) passes around a defender. The height of the ball and Johnson's extended follow-through indicate a full-range pass. To make a pass like this without alerting the defender, you must restrict your preliminary movements to a minimum. Moving the ball from the waist to chest height, and "winding up" the passing arm, give the move away. Strengthen your shoulders, biceps and wrists to be able to pass without exaggerated preparation.

STEP 1
The push pass can be used within the same range as a chest pass; it is also suitable for shorter distances where the ball must not travel too fast for the receiver to be able to control it. Hold the ball in both hands in front of the chest until you make the throw, so defenders won't know what sort of pass you will make or which hand you are going to use. In this example, the player will use his left hand.

STEP 2
The ball is held just above shoulder height, a little to the side, the elbow tucked in. The opposite foot (the right, in this instance) steps forwards, although this isn't necessary for very short passes. To pass around a defender who is close-guarding you, you can step out and forwards with the other foot.

STEP 3
The wrist, cocked naturally to cradle the ball, now snaps forward to release it. Some power comes from the shoulder and elbow, according to the distance required.

PASSING: BOUNCE AND OVERHEAD

1 THE BOUNCE PASS

The basic action for the bounce pass is similar to that used in the chest pass except that the ball is pushed from about waist height, rather than chest height, and the thrust is slightly downwards. Here we see the defender preventing the attacker from using the chest pass by stretching out his arm. The passer's body is crouched slightly and he leans forwards more than he would if delivering the ball from the chest. This low position makes it hard for the pass to be blocked.

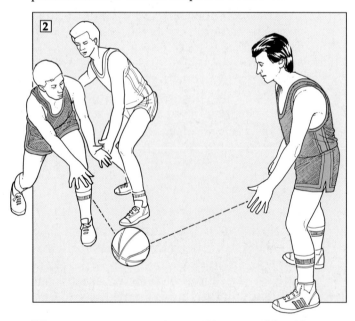

2 The ball should travel as quickly as possible without any loss of control or accuracy. To achieve this, the wrist and fingers snap out of their cocked position to drive the ball across the floor towards an available team-mate. It should reach him in one bounce, the ball striking the floor about three-quarters of the way between the ball handler and the receiver. The ball should reach him no higher than his hips — so aim for a low, skidding bounce.

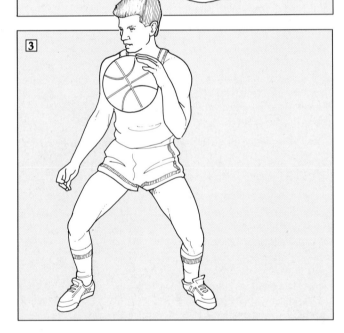

3 At the end of the move the passer's thumbs and palms face the floor. As we have suggested, the pass is effective when the player with the ball is being hampered by a tall defender intent on preventing a shot or high pass. It is also very useful against a zone defence, where attackers have the chance to move in and out of the restricted zone without being closely guarded. A more difficult, one-handed version is an effective way of passing quickly at the end of a dribble.

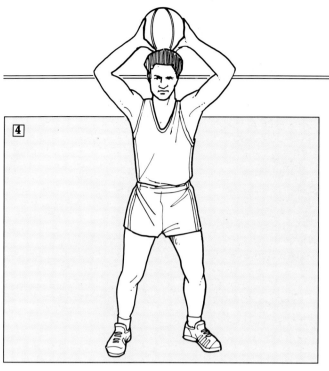

4 OVERHEAD PASS

The two-handed overhead pass has many advantages, particularly for the taller player. Because the passer's position is similar to that adopted for a shot at the basket, the defence will be unsure what they are defending against, and it is easy to fake a shot or side pass before lobbing the ball to a teammate. The ball is held directly over the head, thumbs behind the ball and fingers spread to the side. The player takes a step forward as he releases the ball.

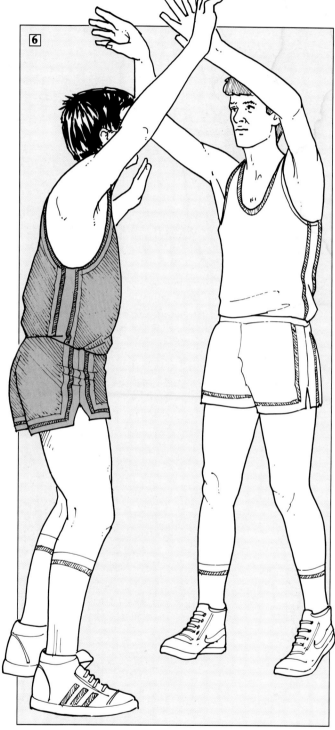

5 The ball is flicked rather than thrown, so most of the force again comes from the snapping motion of wrist and fingers. This pass is best used over short distances. Two or three such passes, used in quick combination, can be a very good way of penetrating a defence. If more distance is needed, some arm movement will be necessary, but this takes away the surprise element of the pass and beginners often find it difficult to judge both the correct strength and direction.

6 Note that the passer has kept his feet on the floor throughout the move. Since the ball is pushed slightly downwards, the fingers and palm end up facing the floor as the wrist completes its follow-through. Beginners often make the mistake of bringing their hands behind their head and pushing from the elbows, with the palms facing forwards at the end of the move; this leads to loss of control and also announces the passer's intentions to the opposition.

SHOOTING: THE SET SHOT

All the techniques explored in this book so far lead to a player getting the ball and shooting at the basket. Several times in the course of the game that player will be you — each team member has the responsibility of scoring. The hoop is twice the diameter of the ball, so you should feel confident. On the other hand, it is 10ft (3m) off the ground and there are five players doing their utmost to ensure that you fail, so you will appreciate that shooting is something that you can never practise enough.

When to shoot? Among the things you should consider are:
- how high are your chances of success?
- is there a team-mate in a better position?
- how many seconds of your half-minute of possession remain?

There are several types of shot, and you should learn them all so you can select the appropriate one. With the exception of the dunk (see photos on pages 34-5), they have many features in common: the fingertips control the ball and the snap of the wrists produces backspin, which slows up the flight, while correct timing of the release and a smooth, relaxed execution produce the arc traced by an accurate ball on its way to the basket. You should look at the target (whether the ring or the backboard) and concentrate fully on the shot. The set shot, described below, is a good shot to learn first.

STEP 1
Hold the ball in the fingers and thumbs of both hands and face the basket, feet placed shoulder-width apart, the right foot slightly forward (or the left foot for left-handers). As you bring the ball up from the chest, turn it so that the shooting hand is underneath and behind the ball, with the other hand supporting the ball at the side. The knees are bent as the ball is raised just above the head. Look at the target. At this stage, the wrist of the shooting hand is bent right back.

STEP 2
The guiding hand is taken off the ball, the legs and arms straighten fully and the wrist snaps as the ball is released. It is usual to go up onto your toes.

STEP 3
The follow-through is important in every shot as it ensures a smooth action and a gentle, arced flight. The set shot is used about 15ft (5m) or more away from the basket when the player has time to make the necessary preparation.

THE FREE THROW
The moment before release; Akeem Olajuwon on the free-throw line. The Houston Rockets player's concentration is absolute as he looks at the target, but there is no evidence of tension. Almost all players these days use the set shot at free throws.

 STAR TIP
Taking a free throw (or two or three free throws) can be a nerve-racking experience, especially towards the end of a close game. Watch players like Akeem Olajuwon and notice how they develop little routines to dissipate nerves. Movement releases tension, that's one advantage; but also by getting into a habit of bouncing the ball once, say, after brushing your forehead with your wristband, you will develop a rhythm which leads naturally into the shot.

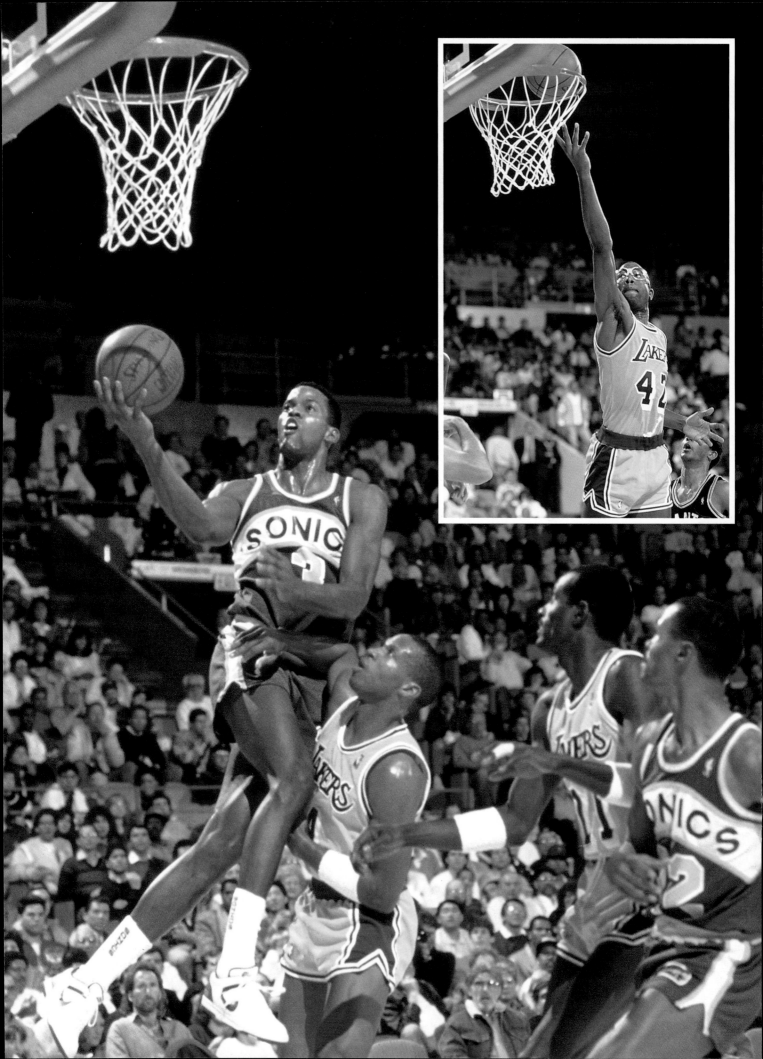

SHOOTING: THE LAY-UP

Many shots are taken on the run, and the co-ordination and timing required to jump and shoot effectively only come with lots of practice. Things become even more complicated if you have just been fed a pass but have no time or room to dribble before the shot. You must catch the ball in your stride and take off without committing a travelling violation.

The lay-up is one shot which follows a dribble or a pass taken on the run, and the "one-two" rhythm used to help you stop before pivoting (pages 18-19) can help you time your jump. More points are scored with this shot than any other in open play. Like nearly all shots in the modern game, it is taken with one hand, and if there is one shot worth learning to execute well with your weaker hand, this is it. The approach is from either side of the basket and the shooting hand changes accordingly, so ambidextrous skills will double your scoring chances with the lay-up. The breakdown which follows is for a shot from the right, so substitute the left hand and foot for the right hand and foot, and vice versa, to make a lay-up from the other side of the basket.

LAY THE BALL ON THE SHELF

That's how the shot got its name: think of the ring as a flat shelf and place the ball on it (with a little help from the backboard on most occasions). Here, Dale Ellis of Seattle is seen on his way up to do just that. Note how he protects the ball by turning his body into the defender: a trick which hasn't helped the opponent with his jumping.

STAR TIP

Sometimes you will be lucky enough to have a free run at the basket down the centre of the court, allowing you to do a lay-up from the front. James Worthy (INSET) of the Lakers shows how it's done. You would be best advised not to use the backboard. Lay up with your hand under the ball and just let it roll off your fingertips into the net.

STEP 1

Once you have caught the ball, whether from a pass or from your own dribble, each foot may touch the floor once only before the shot. The ball is held at about waist level with both feet off the ground, the right foot coming down to land. Count "one" to yourself as it does so. Your left leg follows through for the final step. The run is angled in towards the basket, which is to your left.

STEP 2

The left foot hits the ground (count "two") after a shorter step and you spring upwards off it, your right knee raised to help you gain height. Look at the target and lift the ball up with both hands. Aim to make as high a jump as possible and to keep vertical in the air, as this will help to bring you nearer the target.

STEP 3

The left, supporting, hand comes away from the ball and the right hand stretches up, lifting the ball towards the basket. The hand can be behind the ball or underneath it, whichever suits your style. The ball leaves the fingers and is played gently against the backboard to drop into the basket.

BASKETBALL
OTHER SHOOTING TECHNIQUES

[1] – [6] Slam! The **dunk shot** is the most exciting and dramatic shot in basketball, having all the power and ruthlessness of a smash in tennis or a left hook in boxing. The player has to jump close in to the basket to get his hands above the level of the ring, and then he rams the ball into the net. The difficulty of the shot is compensated for by two huge advantages: once you're up there it's almost impossible to miss, and only a very well-placed defender who has timed his jump to perfection can oppose it. Here are:

[1] Patterson of Leicester (England) meeting no resistance from the Bracknell Tigers' defence on his way up;

[2] Patterson finishing the job;

[3] Ed. Pinckney of the Sacramento Kings getting one in against the opposing team;

[4] Ray Tolbert of the Lakers getting revenge in like fashion;

[5] A.C. Green, also of the Lakers, executing a brilliant one-handed dunk (note the other arm keeping the defender away) against Phoenix;

[6] Finally, "Spud" Webb pulling off an exhibition shot in an All-Stars game — a two-handed reverse dunk.

[7] – [10] The **lay-up**, or **bank shot**, is the staple shot of basketball and should be practised so that its execution is second nature.

[7] In the first shot we have the Boston Celtics' Larry Bird sending the ball towards the backboard from a fair distance.

[8] & [9] The next two photos show the Lakers on the receiving end from Derek Harper of Dallas, and John Williams of Cleveland.

[10] And finally, a good example of a lay-up from directly in front of the basket; the Lakers score here as Bryon Scott lets one roll off his fingertips.

STAR TIP

If a defender gets between you and the basket as you jump to attempt a lay-up from the side, you should respond in the way the players in these photographs would – with a variation known as the **hook shot.** *Instead of turning your body towards the basket, which would give the defender a chance to block the shot, you keep the shoulder of your non-shooting arm next to the defender. This means there are now two bodies between the ball and the target, and you hook the ball high over both, with an exaggerated "putting your hat on" action.*

11 The advantage of being able to improvise: Reggie Theus "spoons-off" a shot from the edge of the key. He still has one foot on the ground and the opposing defence has been taken by surprise.

12 & **13** As you get involved in higher standards of basketball, you will notice that it is rare to get the time to take a **set shot** in open play. It has been replaced by the **jump shot** which can be performed on the run and is more difficult to defend against.

12 The first shot here is by Seattle's Xavier McDaniel who manages to get his attempt in, despite determined opposition.

13 The second has left Bryon Scott's hand before the Phoenix defender has reacted. Note how both players are almost perfectly vertical.

11

12

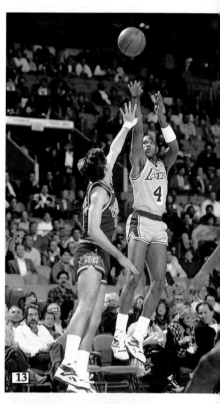

13

14 – **16** The set shot should also be practiced as often as possible – every player has to take free throws and you will feel less pressure if the action has become automatic. On page 30 the shot is broken down into its stages, but of course the execution should be a continuous, flowing motion, with the ball describing a gentle arc. In this sequence Alan Cunningham, the England-based American star, reminds us what a smooth and graceful shot it is.

14

15

16

JUMPING

Consider the activities in basketball which require you to jump:
● intercepting high passes;
● shooting (in most cases);
● blocking shots and high passes from the opponent nearest you;
● winning the ball as it rebounds off the basket or backboard;
● contesting a jump ball.
In addition, it is sometimes necessary to jump in order to receive a pass. Whatever your height or ability, you should strive to improve your jumping because it is something you will have to do in every game and it forms an essential part of basketball, as you will see on pages 38-9. Moreover, if you are involved in a held ball or double foul, you will have to contest the jump ball.

If you are tall and have strong legs, you will have two great natural advantages when it comes to jumping. However, these will count for very little if you are unable to time your jump well; the most common mistake, whether in rebounding or blocking a shot, is taking off too soon. When blocking against the jump shot, only jump when the shooter jumps; otherwise he might fake the shot, watch you jump, and then set off on a dribble. You cannot defend against that very effectively with both feet off the ground! You should stand with feet well apart and knees bent, ready to launch into a jump. Watch how the attacker is holding the ball to get a clue about his intentions.

STEP 1

A jump ball in the centre circle is used to start each period of the match – one player from either team contesting it. If, in the normal course of play, two opposing players appear to knock the ball out of bounds together, then – like those involved in a held ball or a double foul – they must have a jump ball. In such cases, the jump ball takes place in whichever restraining circle is nearest to the incident. The players in the circle stand in their own half, facing the opponents' basket, with a side-on stance and their front foot near the centre line. All the other players must stand outside the circle.

STEP 2

As the ball is thrown straight up, the players' knees are bent, ready to jump. Their arms will come up to give extra lift.

STEP 3

They take off from the balls of their feet, one arm extended for extra reach.

REACH FOR IT
British League players for Solent and Kingston battle it out in a jump ball. Timing is everything in this contest, not only to beat your opponent but also to play within the rules; it is a violation to touch the ball if it hasn't reached its highest point. Reach with one hand only; two hands are used when it is better to catch than to tip, for instance on a defensive rebound.

 STAR TIP
Small players must perfect their timing to compete in jump balls and rebounds. Make sure you touch the ball at the peak of your jump.

REBOUNDING

"Rebounding" is the name given to the jump a player makes to win the ball after it has bounced off the backboard or the ring of the basket following an unsuccessful shot. Clearly, this is a crucial area of the court in which to win possession of the ball, and the determination of the players is always evident. The aim of the attacker is either to regain possession in order to take another shot, or to tap the ball into the basket with the fingertips (the "tip-in"). The defender, ideally, would like to come down with the ball in both hands and launch a counter-attack, either by driving out of the back court or by passing quickly to a free team-mate. Failing that, the defender tries to "bat" the ball away from his basket. Defenders, then, usually jump with two hands up, while attackers use just one and benefit from the extra height this gains them. The tactics used by both teams in the short time between the ball leaving the shooter's hand and the players jumping are also quite different.

The attackers must try to out-smart the defence by speed and deception, and they are at a disadvantage in that the defenders guarding them are nearly always nearer the basket. An attacker winning the ball from a rebound may decide to jump again immediately to shoot — a real test of strength and fitness when nearing the end of a tiring game.

THE PRINCIPLE OF VERTICALITY

Every player is entitled to the space directly above his head. In rebounds, where so many players are jumping in such a limited space, referees are particularly concerned with this principle. Players should not lean forwards or backwards, nor should they jump at an angle. In this photo from the European Basketball Final between Barcelona and Aris, you could imagine a cylinder drawn around each player (the width of his shoulders being its diameter). The cylinders would stand almost parallel without touching.

Who is defending the basket? It must be the Aris player in yellow; only he has two hands up.

STAR TIP

In rebounds, defenders winning the ball should not hold it close to their bodies when they land — that could result in a held ball. Tall players should hold the ball up high; small players should hold it low, away from their torso, with their elbows out.

STEP 1

In rebounds, the defender is usually nearer the basket than his opponent and can get the upper hand by "blocking out" the attackers. This tactic is most effective when carried out against all the opposition, including the player who took the shot. In most cases, a defender will normally be between the basket and the person he is guarding, so when he sees a shot being attempted he will be in a good position to obstruct the forward's path to the basket.

STEP 2

When he sees the route the forward intends to take, the defender pivots so that his back is facing his opponent. Note that if the defender pivoted in the opposite direction, he would almost certainly foul the player. The defender may have to shuffle across if the attacker tries to go round him.

STEP 3

Then it is in for the rebound. Do not jump exactly beneath the basket — if the ball comes down there, it's a basket anyway!

THROW-IN

When the ball goes out of bounds, the team not responsible for the ball going out of play is awarded a throw-in from the sideline, at the point at which the ball crossed the line. A sideline throw is also awarded after a violation (an illegal dribble, for example). The ball is returned to court from the end line by the team defending that basket after they have conceded a basket. The ball crossing the end line in open play results in a throw-in from whichever sideline is nearer the point where the ball crossed, and from a point as near as possible to the end line. However, where National Basketball Association (NBA) rules apply in the United States, the ball is returned to the court from the *end line* at the point it went out of play.

Throw-ins, then, occur several times during a game, so it is worth giving some thought to the possibilities this possession offers. Generally speaking, the nearer a throw-in is to their basket, the more tightly a team will defend against it. A throw from the end line, for example, may not always be immediately opposed, and the defending team might concentrate on assuming a defensive formation in its back court. This is not always the case, especially if the defending team feels it is worth the risk of pushing all its players up. In any case, the team taking a throw-in from its own half should always see whether a fast break is possible.

STEP 1
This player is taking a throw from the sideline, and the opposition is guarding his team-mates very tightly.

The player nearest him wants to receive the ball, but he must first shake off his defender. He starts to move to his left, towards the halfway line, taking the defender with him.

STEP 2
The forward stops, and pushes off his left foot straight away.

At the same time he signals in the opposite direction with both hands. This gesture will be seen by the player with the ball, but not by the defender. The defender is already committed to going in the opposite direction.

STEP 3
The defender is stranded as the ball is thrown to the attacker who brings *both* hands over for the catch.

The passer must see the fake work before passing to the signalling player.

THROW-INS
A standard chest pass side-line throw from Henning Harnisch of Germany's Bayern Leverkusen. Once a player on the court touches the ball, the clock restarts.
INSET: a more casual under-arm flick pass brings the ball into bounds from the end line. You can afford to do that when none of your opponents are near.

 STAR
TIP
Two people are involved in a pass and the receiver very often has to do a lot of work. Hold your hand out to show where you want the pass, but don't call. That would only alert the opposition.

TEAMWORK: DEFENCE (1)

Defence may not seem as exciting as attack, but it has its advantages. You are more mobile and agile when you don't have to concentrate on controlling the ball and moving it around the court, and you don't have to worry about breaking any of the time rules (see pages 62-3) which apply when you are in possession. Besides, good defence is how to get the ball back without conceding a score — and then you can begin your attack again. If the opposition has the ball, it is the duty of every member of your team to defend. The better you defend, the fewer points you have to score to win.

Physical contact is illegal, but you may obstruct the player who has the ball by facing him with both feet on the floor, and then sliding to maintain your guard on him. The player with the ball should always be threatened. Try to knock the ball away if he is dribbling; if you're sure he's going to shoot, stand up straight and raise both arms above your head.

CUTTING DOWN THE OPTIONS
You wouldn't go so far as to say she's trapped, but the Australian player is certainly looking for help, thanks to some good defence work by the Russian. If there are faults, the defender's left knee shouldn't be bent inward and her feet could be wider apart. Note the pivot foot of the attacker.

INSET: here we see some good team defence at the 1989 World Invitation Club Basketball (WICB) Championships at Crystal Palace, England. As Bayern Leverkusen's Clinton Wheeler advances with the ball, Mike Hammond extends his arms and takes up a defensive stance. Paul Cummings checks to see what is happening over to the right, and, barely visible behind Wheeler, another opposing player goes across to the other side towards John Johnson — probably to put a press on him.

STEP 1
The defender has taken up a good stance (see also inset photo on page 16), not so near the dribbler that he can drive past, nor so far back that he can shoot comfortably. You might stand nearer an opponent who is a good shot but cannot dribble well; you would stand further away if the opposite were true. Note that the defender has one hand up and the other down to restrict the outlets available to the attacker. He is between his opponent and the basket, and is concentrating fully on defence.

STEP 2
By good sliding footwork, the defender "overplays" the dribbler, that is, he manoeuvres him away from the basket, towards the sideline. It is worth studying your opponents to find their weaknesses; then you can try to force them to dribble with their weaker hand, by blocking the other side.

Trapping a dribbler in a corner is good defence.

STEP 3
Unsettled by the tenacious defender, the player with the ball has had to stop dribbling; he is now under pressure because, being closely guarded, he has only 5 seconds in which to part with the ball or else concede possession to the opposition.

TEAMWORK: DEFENCE (2)

So far we have concentrated mainly on how to defend against the player with the ball. But what about the other four members of the opposition, all of whom are keen to receive a pass and who are moving into menacing positions in your back court? Various tactics can be used to counter this threat and we shall examine some of them in this section, but first let's state some general principles about team defence: players should inform each other all the time of their own strategies and their opponents' activities; they should be flexible about the systems they use and be prepared to abandon one tactic entirely if it obviously isn't working; and they should match up players — small against small, tall against tall, fast against fast and so on.

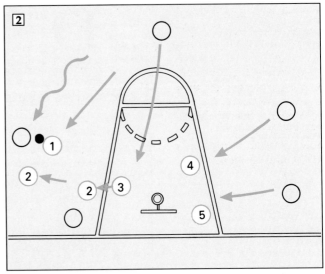

[2] "SAGGING"

Defenders retreat towards their basket until the ball is near their player; then they move up, ready to intercept the pass. If the player with the ball gets free, the nearest player must challenge him, and if he looks like losing possession two men can challenge him — as in this example: here we see the dribbler being "double-teamed" while the other defenders drop back towards the basket, a move known as "sagging".

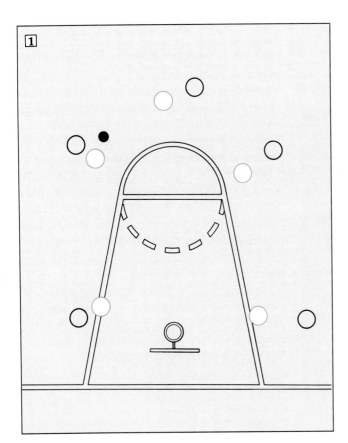

[1] ONE-TO-ONE

In all of these teamwork diagrams the ball is represented by a small circle, attackers by open circles, and defenders by shaded circles. Here we see a one-to-one system where each defender guards an attacker, standing between him and the basket. The player with the ball is guarded closely.

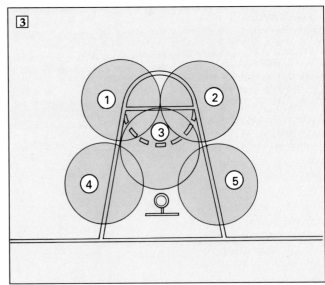

[3] ZONE DEFENCE

Zone defence, used against teams that like to penetrate the key but don't like long-range shooting, gives each player responsibility for an area of the back court about the size of a centre circle. In a 2-1-2 formation, it looks like this. Note the overlaps. The centre of the free-throw line must be guarded. Defenders move towards the ball as a unit. Any attacker getting near the basket is guarded one-to-one.

4 Here the ball is played out wide to attacker 3, and this becomes the new focus. Defender 2 moves to challenge, while the other defenders, still within their areas, move across. The aim is to restrict the opposition to difficult long shots. Note how defender 3 drops back to a central position.

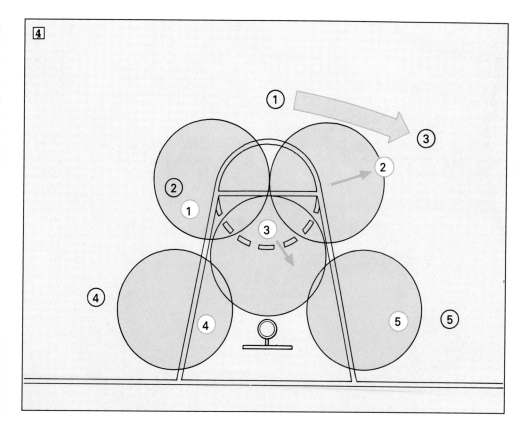

KEY
dribbling player
path of pass
movement of player

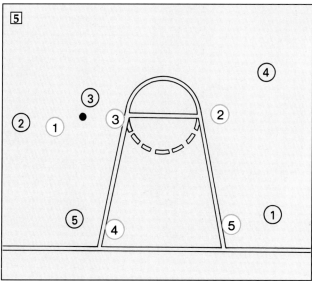

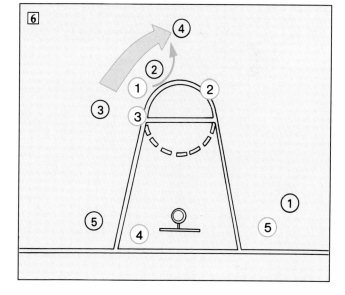

5 "BOX AND ONE"
When the opposition has one particularly skilful player who can win the game for them, you can try to mark him out of the game by putting one player on him permanently. The system shown here is known as "box and one". Defender 1 has the job of making sure attacker 2 doesn't get the ball. It involves a risk because defender 1, intent on cutting out the pass, will not always be fully between his attacker and the basket, which will allow him lots of movement on the blind side.

6 Attacker 3 has passed to 4, and defender 1 must now change his position to place himself between attacker 2 and the ball. The other defenders must be prepared in case attacker 2 gets free, but the player with the ball is the main target.

TEAMWORK: ATTACK (1)

It has been emphasised throughout this book that there is not as much specialisation in basketball as there is in most team sports. Every player must be able to perform all the skills well, and every player is both attacker and defender as required. Having said that, players do adopt certain roles in attack according to their size and natural abilities. Guards, also known as playmakers, tend to be fairly small. They are good ball handlers and passers, fast, driving dribblers, and are capable of long-range shooting. They should also have good tactical awareness.

Guards play at the back of the attack. The forwards play at the sides of the key and shoot from there. They move into the key to help with rebounds. The centres, usually the tallest team members, get as near to the basket as possible. A typical attack would have one guard, two forwards and two centres. In addition to the five players on the court, there may be also a number of substitutes who can be used.

THE PLAYMAKER
A sight most defences fear: Alton Byrd, the Kingston (England) guard and one of the great "generals" of the game, tells his team-mates what positions to take up as he advances towards the Manchester key. The defender, respecting Byrd's dribbling skills, lays off him. This shot was taken at the British Nat-West Final in 1989 where Kingston won 86-77.

STEP 1

Because of his skills, the guard is relied on by his team-mates to set the pattern of an attack. Here we see the guard receiving a pass a few yards from the opposition's free-throw line. A common mistake among beginners is to bounce the ball once they have caught it. If they are challenged strongly, they may have to stop the dribble after one bounce, and the rules do not allow them to restart it. Close marking will then force them to release the ball within 5 seconds. This player still has all possible options before him, including pivoting. He looks around before deciding which action would be best for the team.

STEP 2

A defender moves in to challenge. There are no safe passes the guard can make, and a shot from this range would not have a high chance of success. On the other hand, he is a good enough dribbler to go into a protected dribble while waiting for a good opportunity for attack. As he directs his team-mates, he is aware that there are only so many seconds left before a shot must be made.

STEP 3

Having faked a shot, the guard sends a bounce pass into the key where a forward has made a well-timed run.

TEAMWORK: ATTACK (2)

When you have the ball, shoot if there is a good chance of success and your team-mates are there for the rebound; otherwise, bear in mind that a thrown ball moves more quickly than a dribbled ball. Dribble if a pass is likely to be intercepted, or if a penetrating drive towards the basket is possible. Players without the ball should also be busy. By spreading out, they open up the court to make moves possible. On the other hand, they should be prepared to move towards the player with the ball if he needs help, or to set screens (see pages 50-51). Snappy, accurate passing is effective; the more the ball is moved about, the greater the likelihood of a defensive error. Against a zone defence, attackers should get into receiving positions around the key, and a reliable medium-range shooter can also cause problems.

Another tactic is to get a tall player under the basket. Defences can be broken down by good, aggressive dribbling and players moving into the key for passes. Players without the ball should fake as well, especially when cutting towards the basket. The pattern of attack should be varied, especially if you are having limited success, if the scores are close, or the opposition is beginning to read your game. The guard's position is important, as attack may turn into defence instantly; there should always be one player at the rear of the attack for defensive balance.

STEP 1

The attacker in the white vest is within striking range of the opponents' basket, so she is being guarded closely. She must lose the defender for a second to receive the ball. One option is to fake a run in one direction, and then turn and head off the opposite way. If the defender doesn't react to the fake, she can continue on the original course.

STEP 2

In this case the attacker wants to keep the position she has. She steps back towards the defender so that she places her back foot, the right one in this instance, in front of the defender's front foot. The defender's movements are now limited and the attacker can step forwards and out with the front foot.

STEP 3

As the attacker makes the move, she extends her left arm to show where she wants the player with the ball to pass it. Once she receives the ball, she can pivot off the back foot and face the basket.

ASKING FOR
THE BALL
This shot was taken during the 1989 NatWest Final in the UK. Manchester is posing an impressive man-to-man defence, but Kingston has found a passing lane. The player with the ball is set to make an overhead pass and his opponent is guarding against it with arms raised. The Kingston player in the key, however, has just managed to get away from his guard and is reaching out his left arm to receive a possible bounce pass.

TEAMWORK: ATTACK (3)

A screen is an offensive ploy which takes advantage of the ruling that allows a player to move into any unoccupied space on the court. An attacker stands near a defender in order to prevent him following the path which he would take to guard the player with the ball or the player who is about to receive a pass. Screening requires lots of practise, but it is worth the effort because it is such an effective tactic when done well. Used against a one-to-one defence, it upsets the whole balance of the system. The ideal screen gives the player with the ball an unhindered run to the basket. The screener must be careful not to foul. If he is going to screen a player who is moving, he must allow him space and time in which to stop. If the screen is open, for instance, to the front or side of the defender, and is within his field of vision, the screener may stand as close as possible without making physical contact.

A blind screen is made behind a defender and must be at one running stride's distance from him, giving him room to turn. The defender is advised to stand with his arms crossed on his chest and his legs in the normal defensive stance so that he does not run the risk of committing a foul. Once the screen is set he may not move until the freed player has gone past the screen, unless the screened defender moves and the screener can follow his path. All of this may sound daunting, but essentially it means:

- don't crash into the defender;
- don't block his way with your arms or legs;
- don't prevent him from moving.

Of course, if he forces his way through, he commits a personal foul.

In this section we examine four types of screen used on the left side of the court; each is possible from other directions as well, as shown in diagram 1.

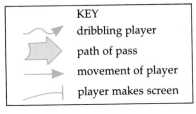

KEY
dribbling player
path of pass
movement of player
player makes screen

1 SPLITTING THE POST
Player 1 passes to player 2, then follows the ball, cutting to the right of 2. Meanwhile, player 3 runs towards player 2 and cuts behind 1 to the left of 2. Attacker 3 should time his run to arrive at player 2 just after player 1. Defenders will find player 2 an obstacle if guarding either cutter. Player 2 can pass to either team-mate by handing, not throwing, the ball (the hand-off or flip pass). Screens may be at any point, as shown.

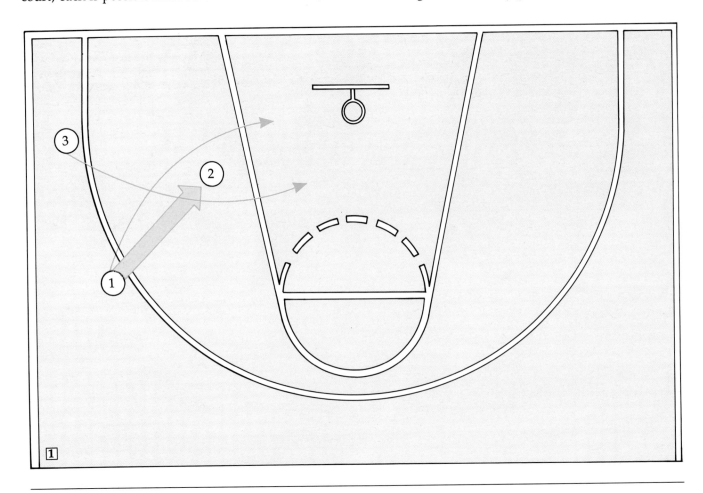

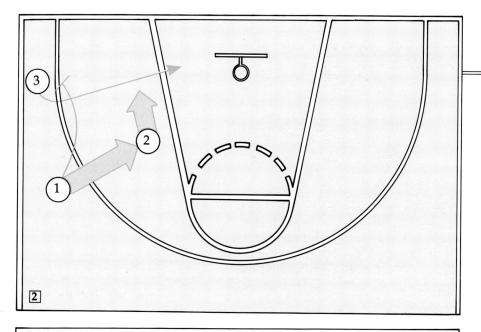

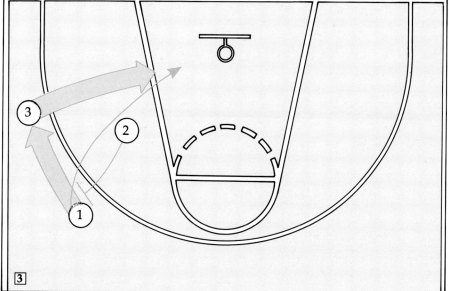

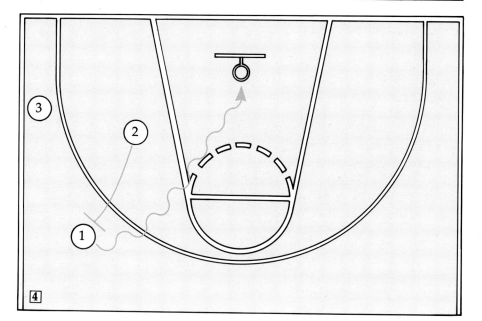

2 SCREEN OFF THE BALL (A)
Player 1 passes to 2, then screens 3 who cuts towards the basket and receives a bounce pass or overhead pass from 2.

3 SCREEN OFF THE BALL (B)
Player 2 screens player 1 after player 1 has passed to 3. Player 1 cuts off 2's screen towards the basket and catches 3's overhead pass.

4 SCREEN ON THE BALL
Player 2 goes towards the player with the ball (1) and screens him so that he can dribble past without being challenged. These last three manoeuvres should result in a lay-up. Cutters should brush the screen as they pass.

Bayern Leverkusen's Clinton Wheeler is free to dribble on, thanks to the screen set by team-mate Günther Behnke. He seems to be hindering Tim Harvey in a less than legal fashion, but when you are 7ft 2in (2.2m) tall, people don't argue with you!

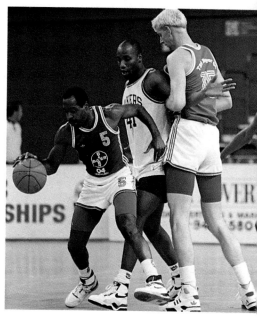

RULES AND ETHICS

The rules of basketball are intended to ensure three main conditions:
- that there is as little physical contact between opposing players as possible;
- that play is as continuous as possible, with frequent attempts to score and no opportunities for time-wasting;
- that the ball is moved about the court using the hands only, and in such a fashion that a skilful opponent always has a chance of winning possession.

As far as the first condition is concerned, it is worth noting that the rule book acknowledges the difficulty of sticking to the letter of the law when 10 players are moving at speed in a small area. A great deal of accidental contact is inevitable, and as long as no advantage is gained, a foul is not always called.

The second condition is dealt with in some detail in the "Time Rules and Scoring" section on pages 62-63.

The third condition forbids a player to run with the ball in his hands, to throw it from hand to hand, or to clutch it in his arms. The skills of dribbling, pivoting, passing, catching and shooting allow players to work within the framework of the rules.

PERSONAL FOUL
This is any foul involving physical contact, such as pushing or holding. The offender faces the scorer's table and raises an arm to have the foul marked against him. The penalty varies according to circumstances; it might be a sideline throw, or it might be from one to three free throws.

VIOLATION
This is any infringement not involving personal contact or bad behaviour (e.g. "travelling"). The penalty is a sideline throw.

TECHNICAL FOUL
This is also logged against the offender — five fouls and he is substituted — and two free throws are awarded. Swearing is an example of such a foul because it is against the spirit of the game. A quick word on ethics: it is possible to be both competitive and sporting. Always shake hands with the other team when the game ends. Respect the officials and your opponents, and you will enjoy yourself.

KEY TO REFEREE'S SIGNALS
A personal foul   B violation
C travelling   D technical foul

WHEELCHAIR BASKETBALL
With some modification to the rules, it is possible for wheelchair athletes to participate in basketball. Players are classified according to disability to ensure fairly balanced teams. The chair is considered part of the player as far as contact rules are concerned, and a player may stay in the opposing key for 5 seconds instead of 3. Here we see Steve Caine, of the English team Oldham Owls, attempting to block a set shot from Nigel Smith of the Milton Keynes Aces in a match from the World Invitation Club Basketball (WICB) Championships in England in 1989.

Wheelchair basketball is played worldwide at both club and international level. Contact your local or national basketball organisation for details about wheelchair basketball in your area.

WHAT DO THE RULES SAY?

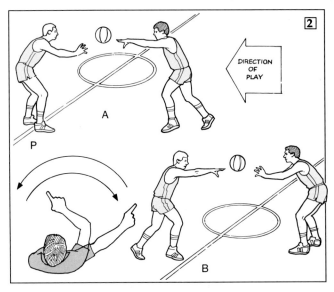

1 INTERCEPTION

Certain areas in the rules of basketball can prove confusing for beginners — and even for more experienced players. In this section, we look at some instances. This first example shows two different shots being intercepted by a defender on the way to the basket. The first instance (A) is against the rules because the shot is on its downward flight and still above the level of the ring. The referee awards the basket (worth 3 points in this case). The second example (B) is within the rules, because the ball is on its upward path.

2 WHEN IS PASSING A VIOLATION?

Both these examples show members of the same team passing to each other. In the first (A), player P has one foot on either side of the halfway line when he receives a pass from the back court. The ball has now moved into the front court, and they need not worry about the 10-second rule (see page 62). In B, we see him passing from the front court. The ball is deemed to have passed into the back court, which is a violation.

3 OUT OF BOUNDS?

In the first picture (A) we see a player standing inside the court but holding the ball over the sideline. Is the ball out of bounds? The answer is "No". In the second example (B), the ball is out of bounds even though it is inside the area of the court, because the player's foot is on the boundary line. The boundary lines do not form part of the playing area and the referee stops the clock prior to awarding a throw.

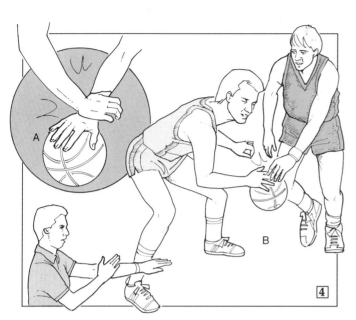

4 FOUL?

The defender in the first picture (A), in trying to dispossess the attacker, hits him on the arm by accident. This is still a personal foul and the other team is awarded a sideline throw. The second picture (B) shows a defender trying to bat the ball away from the attacker, and accidentally hitting his hand in the process. The referee allows play to continue. When a genuine attempt has been made to play the ball, the hand is considered part of the ball, but the arm is not.

6 DUNKING

The first player (A) dunks the ball in the basket, but accidentally hits the ring on the way down. Does the basket count? Yes, it does. In the second picture (B) the player uses the ring to pull himself up to make the shot. In this case the basket would not be allowed and a technical foul would be called.

5 OUT OF REACH

A player is trying to take a throw-in and the defender reaches his arm over the boundary line (A). This is not permitted but the player taking the throw may reach into the court as he does so. This can be best understood by examining the next two pictures. In the first (B), we see the boundary line as the foot of a wall which the players on the court cannot reach through. The last picture (C) shows that the line has a space above it for the player throwing in. Another aspect of the rules might be looked at here. If there is a space of less than 2 yds (2m) behind the boundary line, no player on court can come closer than 1 yd (1m) to the player throwing in.

ACTION STUDY (1)

1 & 2 In this league action from Italy, Alexis of Enimont finds the close attention of Knorr's Bon somewhat restricting. Bon's wide stance and out-stretched arms are limiting the offensive possibilities. Life should always be made uncomfortable for the player with the ball, and the nearer he is to your basket the more you should close him down. Even if he is a good ball-player who can get past you every time with his drib-bling, you should still harass him — there's no point in giving him a free passage to the basket.

A study of defence can also tell you something about attack: Alexis's stance, relaxed with bent knees, means he is mobile and can step into a firm chest pass which Bon can-not intercept.

3 The World Invitation Club Basketball (WICB) Championship, which takes place annually, just after Christmas, involves clubs from all over the world, but it seems fitting that this photo from the 1988 tourna-ment should involve two clubs from the host city of London, England. Brixton, in orange, is attacking the Crystal Palace basket. Note the position of the defen-ders and their response to the shot. The player nearest the shooter jumps in an at-tempt to block the shot. This reaction is automatic and is by no means guaranteed to succeed but, like harassing a dribbler, it is better than no opposition at all. On the far side, the Crystal Palace player is already getting in front of his man to block him out and win any rebound which might result. The

Brixton player on the right is due to find the nearest Palace player moving to block him out also, and the attacker on the free-throw line is also closely attended.

4 It's the Crystal Palace women who are defending here, and the opponents are Oslo of Norway. The player with the ball has been double-teamed and forced to pass back. The other Oslo player is also being closely guarded. Successful double-teaming relies on good tactical judgement and is one of the things that are only truly learnt through match experience. It is risky because it leaves a gap in the defence; on the other hand, it gives you a good chance of winning the ball. Some good dribblers are quite happy to be double-teamed because they are confident

of keeping possession and know that two players on them means no defender on one of their team-mates.

A good time to double-team is when the opposition's 30 seconds are running out, and the player with the ball might be panicked into committing a held-ball violation.

5 & 6 He who hesitates is lost. Another example of double-teaming, this time from the Italian league: Mannion of Vismara fails to move quickly when guarded by the first Phonola player. Gentile seizes the opportunity to double-team and Mannion is closed in on three sides and forced to play away from the Phonola basket.

5

4

6

ACTION STUDY (2)

The importance of practising fundamental skills and maintaining fitness has been stressed throughout this book. Training with the ball, whether alone or with team-mates, is beneficial in several ways, apart from the obvious one of improving your technique. Although its purpose is serious, training can be fun and relaxed at times. A good coach will appreciate the value of allowing players to "let go" once in a while; a player can develop confidence and technique through the occasional practice session in which errors go uncriticised. If you are your own coach, be adventurous in training — although not at the expense of basic skills. It is better to try out fancy dribbles and difficult shots in the gym or in the playground where a mistake is negligible than in a match where points are at stake.

This brings us on to match play. Of course you will play matches in practice but, no matter how competitive they (or you) are, they will never feel the same as a league or cup game. If you get serious about basketball, you will soon appreciate that you can't beat match experience to increase your ability. As well as giving some pointers on defence, the photos and text in the preceding section should have given you some of the *feel* of match play; the intensity, the excitement, the speed at which players have to react. This last point helps to explain what sportsmen mean when they talk about "match fitness". The only true preparation for match play is — match play. It is the only way you will really learn, for example, the shots which have evolved as a consequence of sharp defending, shots like the dunk and the jump shot. In a match, although not every match, you will produce play you didn't think yourself capable of; everyone does. The following studies might help explain why.

STAR TIP

The further you have to bend your knees in order to jump, the more you will warn the opposition of your intentions and the longer it will take you to get off the ground. Practise jumping with minimum knee-flexing.

1 & **2** The advantage of quick reactions. Patterson of Leicester (England) has three Bracknell defenders around him, but his quick take-off gives him an unopposed shot at the basket.

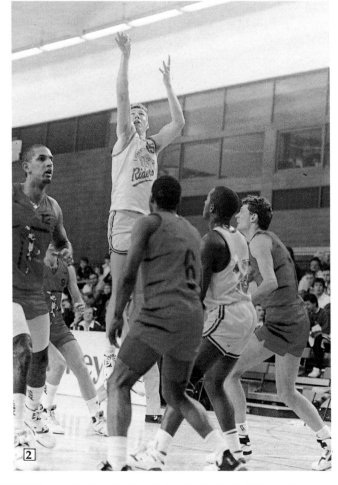

3 – 5 From the same match, Jennings gets away from his man. Once within range of the basket, he bends his knees – a sign that he might try a jump shot (of course he could be faking). He has been quick enough to take the Bracknell defenders by surprise. As in the previous example, the defenders still have their feet on the ground when the ball is released.

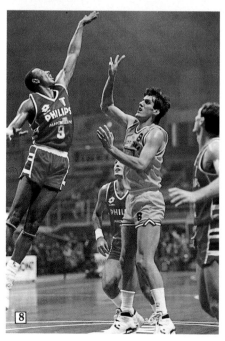

6 – 9 This sequence from Europe shows the kind of competitive pressure you get in top-class matches. Tomic of Yugoplastika is apparently unguarded at the Philips' free-throw line, coiled, ready to take a jump shot. Almost immediately he is challenged, Cureton jumping to block with his hands up. The third picture shows Cureton at the peak of his jump – a fraction of a second earlier and he might have stopped the ball. In the final frame (9), Tomic watches his shot as two more defenders move in for the rebound. But just look at Cureton; even in mid-air he has turned his head to watch the ball.

MENTAL APPROACH

Much is made of psychology in sport these days, and the part played by the mind is generally acknowledged to be an important one. A lot of it, of course, is common sense, but confidence and the right attitude can suddenly seem very distant things, and your body can feel very tired when your team is 15 points down with 2 minutes left, no time-outs remaining, and the team's spirit has dropped — especially if you haven't played particularly well yourself.

In such circumstances, the simplest advice can be hard to remember, let alone put into practice. Perhaps at this point it would be worth reminding ourselves that the mind and body are linked. If you are fit, have warmed up properly and are therefore not worried about injuries, you will have a much more positive attitude on court, and problems will not seem so great. You might even start to enjoy the challenge of containing that really tricky dribbler the other team had the nerve to bring along! Many, many basketball games are won or lost in the last 5 minutes, when players are tired and concentration drops.

Believe that you can win, but on the other hand respect the other team enough not to let up when you're ahead. And if things don't go right, beware of trying too hard; this makes the muscles tense, so they can't do what they would do naturally.

VISUALISATION
If a skill has become automatic, fine. But some moves that you can do in training may seem difficult in a match. Imagining the shot or pass succeeding as you execute it can help. The muscles have a sort of memory of their own and a mental image of the move prompts them to perform in the right way.

TEAM SPIRIT
You can't win the game on your own. Encourage your team-mates and praise good play. On the other hand try to make sure mistakes aren't repeated; but don't criticise needlessly. Nothing encourages a team more than the sight of the opposition bickering among themselves. Captains take note!

EVEN THE BEST PLAYERS MISS
Forget your mistakes and remember your successes. The best way of wiping out an error is by concentrating on the rest of the game and playing well. In a high-scoring game like basketball there are always lots of misses. If the shot is there, take it.

THE RIGHT ATTITUDE
Zan Tabak of Yugoplastika shows the right competitive spirit in a European Cup Final. It could be one of the reasons his team came away with the trophy.

 STAR TIP
If things start going badly in a game, go back to basics: simple, accurate passes; good running off the ball; helping defence whenever necessary; shooting the good percentage shots; and competing for everything. Sometimes teams overcomplicate the game and get themselves in trouble.

TIME RULES AND SCORING

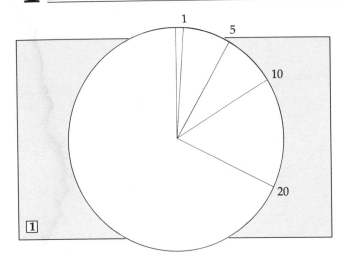

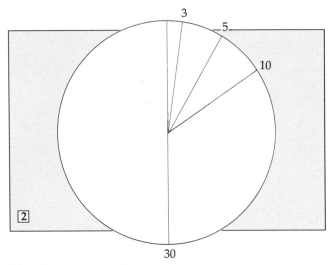

1 PLAY TIME

This hour clock shows the important periods of time which the timekeeper will be concerned with recording, and of which the players must be aware. Each half lasts for 20 minutes of actual play. Then there is a 10-minute interval. If there is a draw after 40 minutes, an extra 5-minute period is played. A draw after this time means another 5 minutes, and so on until there is a clear winner. In each half, both teams are allowed to call two charged time-outs of 1 minute each (and one each for every period of overtime) in which they receive fresh instructions from the coach, discuss tactics — or just get their breath back. These time-outs are not deducted from the 40 minutes of play.

2 VIOLATION TIME

This minute clock shows the time periods concerned with violations. No player, with or without the ball, may stay in his opponents' restricted area for more than 3 seconds at a time while the ball is in his team's possession. A closely guarded player may not hold the ball for more than 5 seconds. This is also the longest time a player has in which to return the ball to court or take a free throw. A team in possession must move the ball into the front court within 10 seconds and, having done so, may not return the ball to the back court. In addition to this, a team must try to score within 30 seconds of gaining possession. In league games a clearly visible clock, which is reset by the 30-second operator when necessary, shows how much of this half-minute remains.

3 THREE POINTS

The referee (A) signals to the scorer that this shot is being made from beyond the three-point line. If the shot is successful (B), it will be worth three points and the referee will raise his other arm with the same signal.

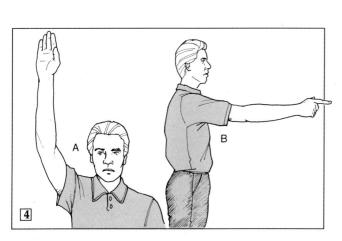

[5] TWO POINTS
Here the referee signals a successful basket worth two points because it was shot from inside the three-point line.

[6] FREE THROWS
Awarded for rule infringements and worth one point each, free throws are taken unopposed from behind the free-throw line. Here, in a nutshell, are how many free throws are awarded, and when:

[4] REFEREE'S SIGNALS
Signal A tells the timekeeper to stop the clock and is used when play is interrupted — by a foul, for example, or a held ball. This is to prevent time being wasted. Signal B tells the 30-second operator to reset the clock because the possession period has restarted.

KEY TO REFEREE'S SIGNALS
A one free throw
B two free throws
C three free throws
D one-and-one

- for intentional fouls, disqualifying fouls, multiple fouls — two free throws;

- on a player shooting (also for personal fouls on player shooting) — if shot went in, one throw plus the basket score; if it failed to go in, two throws (for two-point attempt) or three throws (for three-point attempt);

- for technical fouls — two free throws;

- for personal fouls (not on the shooting player) when the team has seven fouls against it in one half and is not in possession (one-and-one rule) — one throw, followed by another if the first is successful.

FITNESS AND TRAINING (1)

It is impossible to exaggerate the importance of proper warming-up before any exercise (this goes for a match, a training session, or any other form of basketball). Also, proper warming-down afterwards (ideally to be repeated 30 minutes later) is important in order to avoid injury. That is why the first exercises shown here are *a few* of the stretches you should do before doing anything else. Stretching should be gentle and sustained, and not painful. Do not bounce up and down or jerk the muscle. After the initial stretch, repeat the exercise; you should be able to stretch a bit further. Then do some light jogging. In all, 10 minutes should be spent on this before-and-after exercise.

Jumping, so important in basketball, employs the same muscular movement that is used by Olympic-style weight lifters in high pulls and power cleans. You could benefit from some of their training techniques, such as bent-over rowing, tricep extensions and wrist curls. Young children, however, should never use weights. Even if you are old enough, always take expert advice. Agility can be improved by forward and backward runs and skipping. Adults and older children can jog to increase stamina.

The rest of this section deals with circuit training without the ball. Here is how it works: for each exercise see how many sequences you can do in 30 seconds, and halve it for your score. Take a minute's rest between each exercise. Next time you train, do your score for the four exercises (one circuit) three times without a rest, and see how long it takes. Your target is to reduce that time by a third. Retest yourself when you reach it, or after six weeks. Add to or reduce the circuit if you feel like it, but never reduce the *quality* of the exercise.

1 STRETCHING
Wear a tracksuit if it is cold. Stretches A-E should be done twice before running, or playing a game, or training. Stretches A and F-H should be done afterwards.

KEY
A 30 seconds
B 15 seconds each side
C 30 seconds each leg
D 20 seconds each leg
E 20 seconds each leg
F 30 seconds each leg
G 30 seconds each leg
H 30 seconds each leg

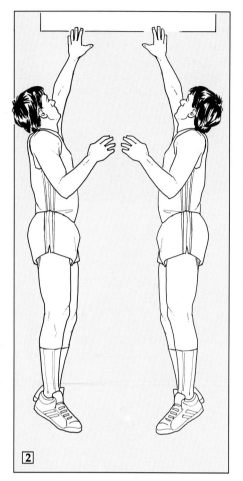

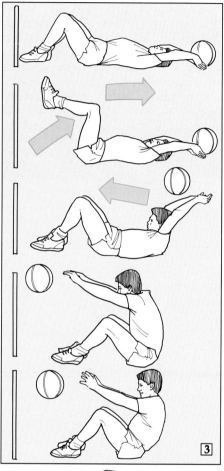

2 ONE SEQUENCE OF REBOUNDING

Under a basketball backboard or something of the same height, jump and touch it with one hand, jump straight back up and touch with the other hand, then with both hands.

3 ONE SEQUENCE OF SIT-UP WITH MEDICINE BALL

Facing the wall, lie on your back with your knees bent, feet on the floor and the medicine ball above your head. Bring your knees towards your hands, then let your feet return to the floor, bringing the ball forward as you do so. As you complete the sit-up, throw the ball against the wall and catch it. If you have no medicine ball, use a basketball or a soccer ball.

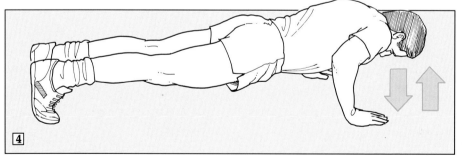

4 ONE SEQUENCE OF PRESS-UP

Lie on your front, toes on the floor, palms of hands flat on the floor next to the shoulders. Press up, keeping body straight. Return to start position with your torso 3in (8cm) off the floor.

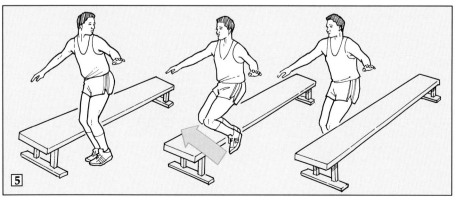

5 ONE SEQUENCE OF SKI-JUMP

Stand sideways next to a bench about 18in (45cm) high. Jump sideways over it, with knees and feet together.

FITNESS AND TRAINING (2)

In this section we look at exercises which can be put together to make a circuit for training with the ball. (Having said that, the first exercise doesn't use the ball at all to begin with!) Find the level of difficulty for each exercise which suits you, i.e. not so hard that it causes frustration, but not so easy that you are not pushed into improving your skills. As you improve, increase the difficulty of the exercise.

1 SHUTTLE RUNS

The shuttle runs in this exercise are for the speed and agility necessary on a basketball court. If you are not on a court, put down your own markers at the same spacing. Run from A to B, turn and run back again, then to C and back to A and so on up to E and back to A. Then do it dribbling a ball with your strong hand. Repeat using your weak hand. Then do it changing the hand used as you turn each time.

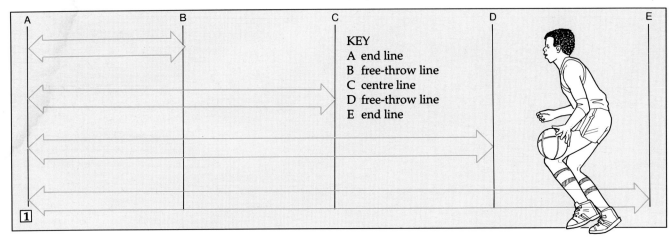

KEY
A end line
B free-throw line
C centre line
D free-throw line
E end line

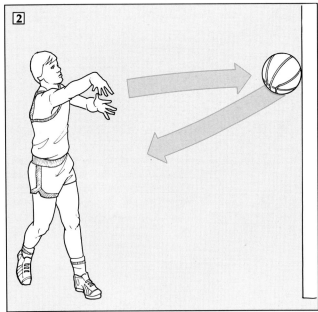

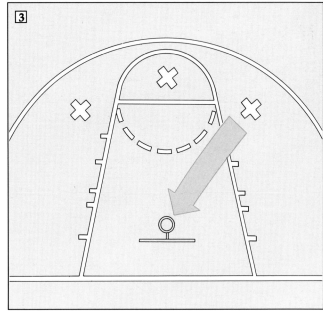

2 PASSING PRACTICE

Run towards the end wall and pass the ball off it to yourself, practising the stride stop and the jump stop as you catch it. Do ten of each. Then do the same off the side wall. Do ten of each. If you have a partner, you can pass to each other instead of using walls. Reduce or increase the number of repetitions according to fitness and ability.

3 SPOT SHOTS

Take five shots from each point. Note your score and try to improve it. Variations include:
- take three shots from each spot using your weak hand;
- make two of the shots from your best distance, the third from your worst position.

4 LAY-UP PRACTICE

Starting from one end of the court, run the full length of the court passing the ball to yourself off the wall (or exchanging passes with a partner running alongside you) and finish with a lay-up. Keep your position(s) and do the same on the way back, thereby practising passing to both sides and shooting with either hand. Do four shots. Then take five free throws, allowing yourself 5 seconds to take each one. (Note how hard it is to be accurate when you are short of breath – this happens in a game.)

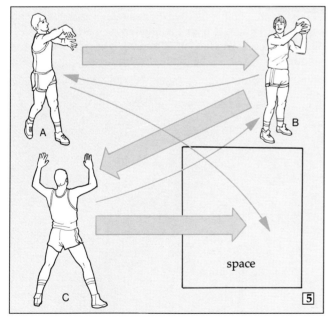

5 PASS AND MOVE INTO SPACE

This requires three people. A passes to B and runs into a space. B passes to C and runs to fill the space vacated by A. C passes to A and fills the space vacated by B. Do this non-stop for 30 seconds. Increase the distance between you as you improve. You must be careful not to get hit by the ball as you run to your new position. Start by using the chest pass and then try the bounce pass and the overhead pass. If you only have one partner, you can practise by passing to each other and then sprinting to certain markers to receive the next pass.

6 DRIBBLING AROUND OBSTACLES

Have the obstacles fairly well spaced out to begin with. Dribble the length of the gym (or two widths) with each hand. Then do two lengths (four widths) changing hands (the crossover) at each obstacle.

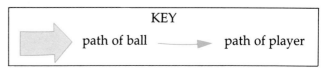

KEY

path of ball ——→ path of player

TESTING YOURSELF

This programme gives you the chance to measure your improvement. Keep a record of your performance and when you start to find that each exercise becomes easier, move on to the next stage.

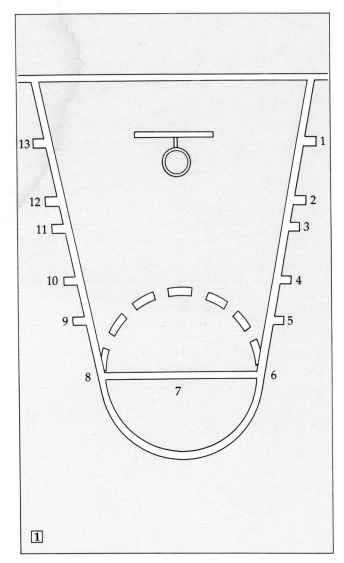

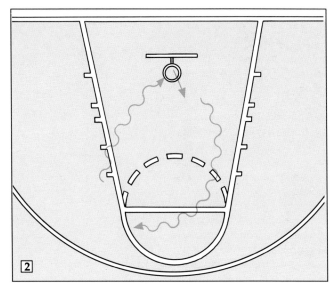

2 LAY-UP
Stage 1: run in from the top of the key dribbling the ball, do the lay-up, collect the ball and return to the free-throw line and repeat. Do five shots, concentrating on accuracy and the "two-count rhythm". Repeat from the other side using your weaker hand. Then take five free throws, each taking no longer than 5 seconds from the moment you are in position.
Stage 2: the same routine, but also do five lay-ups with either hand from straight on, before the free throws.

1 SHOTS AROUND THE KEY
Stage 1: starting at the first spot, shoot at the basket until you succeed (use the set shot). Then move on to spot 2 and do the same, and so on. Keep a score of how many shots you miss. At the end, check your total.
Stage 2: when you have got this down to five misses, move the spots back a yard, and repeat the exercise. Again, get your score down to five misses.
Stage 3: move back another yard and do the 13 baskets using the jump shot.

3 PASSING
Stage 1: with a partner or using a wall, do as many chest passes in 30 seconds as you can from a comfortable distance.
Stage 2: increase the distance by a third and aim to get in the same amount of passes in 30 seconds as you did in stage 1.
Stage 3: as for stage 1 but with bounce passes.
Stage 4: as for stage 2 but with bounce passes.

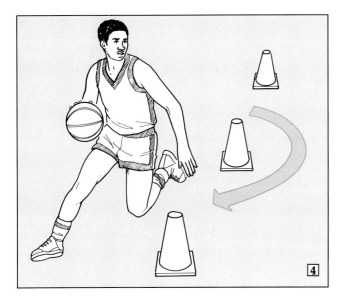

4 RUNNING PASSES

Stage 1: run the length of the gym with a friend, chest passing to each other from a comfortable distance. Only take one stride with the ball, do not dribble. On the return run you will have to use your other hand. Time the two lengths.

Stage 2: increase the distance between you by a third and aim to do the drill in the same time.

Stage 3: as for stage 1 but using bounce passes.

Stage 4: as for stage 2 but using bounce passes. You can practise on your own by using the side walls of a gym.

5 DRIBBLING

Stage 1: dribble straight up and down using your good hand, passing close to the obstacle but not touching it. Repeat, using your weaker hand.

Stage 2: approach the obstacle so that your dribbling hand is the furthest from it. As you pass it, cross over with one bounce to your weaker hand and then back to your good hand. On the way back, start with your weaker hand.

Stage 3: put down more obstacles and dribble in and out, crossing over at each obstacle. Remember to use opposite hands on the return journey.

Stage 4: repeat all these against the clock. This drill also improves peripheral vision.

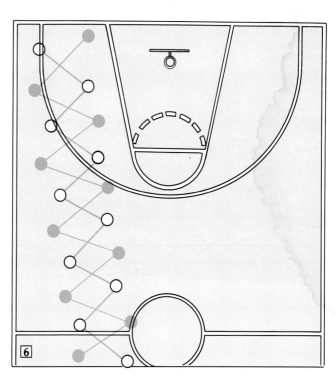

6 ONE-TO-ONE DEFENCE

Stage 1: try to keep between partner (without ball) and basket as he zigzags down the court. Swap roles.

Stage 2: repeat with the ball, ball handler shooting at the end, defender blocking out, both going for rebound.

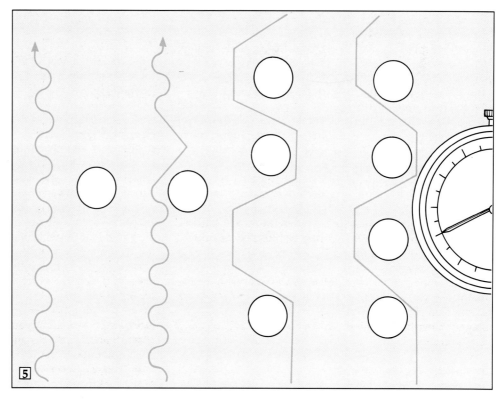

GLOSSARY

Back court – the half of the court which your team defends.

Backboard – rectangular board behind the basket which allows the ball to bounce into the basket or back into play.

Basket – the target; the ball must enter through the circular opening at the top. A net hangs from the ring and slows the descent of the ball so that it can be seen to have scored. A basket is also the name given to a successful shot; it may be worth one, two or three points.

Bat – to knock the ball away using the flat of the hand.

Blocking – personal contact which impedes the progress of a player with or without the ball. This is against the rules.

Blocking out – when a defender positions himself to prevent an attacker getting to a rebound.

Blocks – the marks on the sides of the keys which indicate where the other players should stand while a free throw is being taken.

Bounce pass – a pass bounced once across the floor.

Box and one – a four-man zone defence with the fifth player marking a particular opponent one-to-one.

Centre – an attacking player, usually tall, who takes up a position near the basket.

Chest pass – the basic pass, used over a medium range

when there is no opponent between the passer and the receiver.

Counter-attack is a quick attack launched from a team's own half as soon as it has regained possession of the ball.

Cross-over – bouncing the ball off the floor from one hand to the other while dribbling.

Cut – a quick movement by an attacking player without the ball towards the opposition's basket.

Cutter – player who executes a cut.

Defensive balance – when in attack, there should always be someone in the rear in case there is a quick break by the opposition. This person is usually the guard; if he drives for the basket, another forward should drop back to cover.

Disqualifying foul – a foul bad enough to warrant a player being dismissed for the rest of the match.

Double foul – two opposing players fouling each other at the same time.

Double team – two defenders taking on the player with the ball. In this photograph we see Pittis of Italy being double-teamed.

Dribble – moving the ball around the court by bouncing it off the floor using one hand at a time.

Drive – a fast, aggressive dribble towards the basket.

Dunk – a spectacular shot

in which the player leaps up and rams the ball into the basket from above. Here we see a fine example by James Worthy.

Fake – a move intended to deceive an opponent about your intentions. Sometimes called a feint or dummy.

Forward – an attacking player who operates on the side of the key.

Foul – an infringement which involves physical contact or unsporting behaviour. There are different categories and these are listed separately.

Foul markers – indicators used by the scorers to show how many fouls a player has committed and to show if a team has committed seven fouls in one half.

Free throw – a penalty shot taken unopposed from the free-throw line and worth one point.

Front court – the half of the court your opponents are defending.

Guard – also known as the playmaker, this player is skilful and usually quite small. The guard plays at the rear of the attack. Guard also means to mark an opposing player. In the photograph, the dribbling skills of Tiit Sokk of the Soviet Union draws three French defenders towards him as he directs his team-mates from the top of the key.

Held ball – when two or more opposing players are holding the ball at the same time. There is also held ball in special situations:

(1) ball lodged between the backboard and the ring;
(2) two opposing players knocking the ball out of bounds;
(3) a closely guarded player failing to release the ball within 5 seconds.

Hook shot – variation on the lay-up in which the ball is hooked over the player's head from the side.

Intentional foul – deliberate personal foul.

Jump ball – used to start each period of the game and to restart play after a double foul or a held ball, except special situation (3) above. The referee throws the ball up between two opposing players who jump for it. Here we see a jump ball contested by Janice Lawrence of the USA and Qing Liu of China.

Jump shot (Scoop shot) – variation on the set shot in which the player jumps and releases the ball from a height.

Jump stop – landing with both feet on the floor at the same time as you catch the ball on the run; this allows you to choose your pivot foot.

Key – the restricted area in front of the basket. It is named after its keyhole shape.

Lay-up is the most common shot in open play; the player jumps up and "lays" the ball as if putting it on a shelf. It usually goes in off the backboard.

Multiple foul – two or more players from the same

team committing a personal foul against the same opponent.

One-to-one defence – in this system each defender marks a specific opponent.

Out of bounds – the area outside the court; it includes the lines, the back of the backboard and the supports. A player or ball in contact with the floor in this area is out of bounds.

Overhead pass – a short-range pass played over an opponent.

Overplaying the dribbler – close-marking a dribbler so he cannot go where he wants to but ends up in a disadvantageous position.

Overtime – a basketball game cannot end in a draw, so if scores are equal after 40 minutes, there is an extra 5-minute period known as overtime. If scores remain equal, there are additional 5-minute periods until a clear winner emerges.

Personal foul – a foul involving personal contact against an opponent.

Pivot – when the player with the ball moves his non-pivot foot in any direction while having the pivot foot firmly planted on the floor.

Playmaker – another name for the guard; this name acknowledges the organising and tactical abilities of the player.

Points – the score is registered in points. Free throws are worth one; field goals are worth two, unless shot from outside the three-

point line, in which case they are worth three.

Press – a type of defence where players try to stand between opponents and their team-mate with the ball and mark each player closely.

Push pass – a short or medium-range pass from about shoulder height.

Rebound – jumping and catching the ball after an unsuccessful shot has bounced off the backboard or ring.

Restraining circles – the circles at the top of each key and in the centre of the court. Only two players are allowed in these when a jump ball is in progress.

Restricted area – the area in front of each basket; attacking players may not stay more than 3 seconds in their opponents' restricted area while their own team has the ball.

Sagging – a defensive move

Tiit Sokk of the USSR displays his skill during a match against France.

in which a player moves away from the person he is marking and drops towards the basket.

Scoop shot – see jump shot.

Screen – an offensive device whereby a player prevents a defender from challenging the player with the ball by obstructing his path.

Set shot – a basic shot, used in free throws. Here we see one being taken by Vescori of Italy.

Steal – taking the ball away from an opponent.

Stride stop – stopping a run in one pace while catching the ball and landing with feet astride.

Substitutes – each team has the option of substitutes. These may come on to replace injured players, or

players who have been sent off for committing five fouls. They may also replace a player for tactical reasons.

Team – 10 players, but only five on the court at any one time.

Technical foul – a foul which is against the spirit of the game and doesn't involve physical contact.

Time-out – a one-minute break from play in which teams can plan their game. Each team has two in each half, and is allowed one for every period of overtime.

Travelling – moving with the ball illegally.

Violation – an infringement which does not involve physical contact and is not a technical foul, for example travelling, ball out of bounds, or illegal dribble.

Zone defence – a system in which each defender is responsible for guarding an area rather than a player.

INDEX